Creating A Personal Brand Called You

How to create and build a brand for you

and your business

Debbie Cummings

ISBN: 0615844375
ISBN 13: 9780615844374

Dedication and Acknowledgement

First, I thank God for giving me the skills and talents I have, for giving me the opportunities to effectively use them. For strength and perseverance to continue to push through every step.

This book is dedicated to my two amazing sons, Stephen and Sean, who are my true inspiration in life to be the best I can be, the only two perfect things I have ever done. To my mother who has always believed in me, who motivated me to reach for and achieve my dreams. To my brother, Michael, and his wife, Carol, for being there for me. My nephews, David, Kevin and Andy. To my dad for supporting me and listening.

It is also dedicated to my friend, mentor and coach Jennifer Nicole Lee, a true angel, who has given me her guidance, support and the gentle push and prodding to write this and to make changes in my life. My journey with her has been one of self-discovery and freedom to be who I have always wanted to be. This book would not be here without her.

To all my JNL Fusion sisters for being there, supporting me, pushing me when I didn't think I could continue down this journey. I especially want to thank Agatha Kolodziejczak, Peggy Caruso, Candi Taylor, Rhonda L. Moore and Rula Kanawati for being there for me. Thanks to Alex Gonzalez for the photo shoots and for the beautiful picture on the cover of this book.

I dedicate this to my friend and mentor Nick Lenoci, who has always believed in my talents, and helped me break out of the corporate world. To my best and dearest friend, Marianne Cronin, who stands by me no matter what. My friend Lisa Hynes whose bright smile always helps me get through. Arden Piazza who friendship and support especially over the past year has really helped me shape my future. To my new friend Lorrie Remington for coming along at the right time with the right opportunity to change my life. And to the one who has always been and will forever live in my heart, especially during my most difficult time, assuring me I got this easy ride. I would never have made it through any of this without you.

Thank you to my new found friends in Girls Standing Together, who give me strength and a sense of purpose in the community. I especially want to thank Glenda Chancy for bringing it all together, for being a friend when she didn't know who I was. To Dian Loza, Patricia Scherer, Mary Tiffany, Shirley Stamper and Jennifer Hough Cruise for all you do to make the community and the women of GST better.

In memory of Wendy Chant for starting me on my path to living my passion. I miss you every day.

This book is dedicated to anyone who wants to define themselves, to market themselves, either in the corporate world or to help break out of that world and go out on your own. You are already your own personal brand. Use this book as your beacon to really defining it and building who you are meant to be.

Life truly is a journey and every day is a new path. With faith and patience, everything you need will come to you at the perfect time. May this book help you along that path.

Table of Contents

Forward by Jennifer Nicole Lee

Debbie Cummings is a branding and marketing force to be reckoned with. We met through my JNL Fusion exercise DVD's, from her attending my events, and now we are solid confidants and very close friends. She not only is a marketing maverick, but most importantly an amazing mother and friend to everyone who meets her. To know Debbie is to love her. She has a heart of gold, and a billion dollar brain, with a healthy body to round off the total package of a super successful woman who is in control and in charge of her life.

I had the pleasure of first meeting Debbie at my 2013 JNL World Conference. She had this special sparkle in her eye, and I always knew she was razor sharp in many ways. The conference lit her inner spirit on fire, and her creative energy started to really wow us! To further her career, she made a special visit up to the "Big Apple", and enjoyed one of my world famous Fitness Model Factory 1 Day mega events. Knowing the importance of personal brand and image, she made it a goal to capture gorgeous photos of her in various aspects of her career: fitness, business, and lifestyle. The photos are a powerful sign of her inner strength. And you can tell when you look at these photos her body language expresses the immense wealth of information she has to offer us all.

After we enjoyed the photo shoot, I encouraged her to focus on her dreams and make her goals of authoring a book on branding and marketing a reality. Then we went to work! And boy was it fun! It didn't happen overnight, but now you are holding in your hands right now the very end result of what happens when you dream and dream big.

Just the notion, that one idea of Debbie becoming a published author is now not a dream, or a thought, but a reality!

Debbie is also an amazing key note speaker. I invited her to speak at the 4th Annual JNL World Conference and she enlightened our international group of VIP attendees from all over the world with her knowledge on branding.

What I noticed with Debbie is that she had the priceless branding experience from working with countless companies over the past twenty plus years. This kind of expertise you cannot get from a University. She earned her knowledge from being in the field, day in and day out, designing campaigns and making them work.

In closing, Debbie is an outstanding executive coach and as well as a master personal brand strategist.

Congrats in purchasing and reading this book, as no matter what level you are at in your business and personal branding, you will walk away empowered & enlightened to build your best personal brand ever!

Never give up,

Jennifer Nicole Lee-*Bestselling Author, Creator of the JNL Fusion Workout Method, & CEO of JNL Worldwide, Inc.* **www.JNLMethod.com**

Introduction

Unless you have absolute clarity of what your brand
stands for, everything else is irrelevant.
– *Mark Baynes, Global Chief Marketing Officer, Kellogg Co*

I have spent my entire career building my personal brand, and I've been successful at it. People in my industry know me. Groups and organizations that I work with know me by my work, by my reputation for what I know, for the quality of work I produce and for my work ethic and integrity. I know who I am, what I'm good at, what I love doing. I have always been laser focused on being successful in the job I was in, while keeping my eye on that next step and what I had to do to get there. With every promotion, every project, my brand grew stronger.

When I first thought about going out on my own, what proved to be the hardest thing for me was really defining and branding myself outside the comfort of the corporate world. I knew what I wanted to do, what I was good at, what I wanted to offer. I asked myself a lot of questions that you are probably asking yourself if you are considering starting a business or trying to figure out what you want to be or do. How do I go about turning my passion, my talents into a real business? Where do I start? What do I call my business that would be meaningful to people? How do I differentiate myself and stand out from the others that are offering either the same, or variations of what I really wanted to do or offer? How do I make it memorable enough that people choose me when they need the services that I offer? How do people find out about me? How do I make myself searchable in search engines like Google, and more importantly, how do I make sure that they click to go to my website or my ad? What really surprised me was how much I struggled with this step – coming up with the name that would resonate, the logo that would stand out, the right colors, the right look. And I've been doing branding for years.

I took the time to talk with others who had either expressed an interest in starting a business, and to those who had already started a business, and found a common theme. While they had the passion for their business, knew what they wanted to do, what service or product they wanted to offer, they too struggled with how to develop and build their brand and how to define it. But unlike me, none of them had the expertise or training in branding. It was through these conversations that the idea for this book came to me. How do I take all my years of experience and lessons learned, all the books, the articles, the information I've read and share with others who have the same aspirations as I do to build a business but who struggle with bringing it to life, making it real.

When my life situation changed, I started looking at myself more, trying to figure out what was missing, who I was. I realized that I am my own personal brand, no matter what job I had, what title I carried. They all brought me to where and who I am today – a mother, a business woman, a friend, a marketer, a writer, an entrepreneur wannabe. I don't have to be just one of these to be a brand. It is the whole package – who I am, what I have built myself to – that is my personal brand. Now the challenge is to figure out where I go from here. How I share what I have learned with others to help them find and build their personal brand.

It is my hope and my goal that reading this book will help you on your journey of discovering your personal brand, for whatever reason you want to create one. You can use this to navigate through the corporate world, in a smaller business or to grow your own business. Some parts may be relevant, some not, to your journey, but I consider this book a success if you find even a single golden nugget in here that changes your life and helps you on your path to finding and building your personal brand.

What is a Brand and why do you need one?

It's this simple: You are a brand. You are in charge of your brand.
There is no single path to success. And there is no one right way to
create the brand called You. Except this: Start today. Or else.
Tom Peters, *Author of "In Search of Excellence"*

There is so much talk everywhere about needing a brand. Countless articles and books have been written about this topic. My goal with this book is to create a single resource for you to define, develop, build your brand, and ultimately grow your brand into a successful business. First, let's start with what a brand is and why you need one. I want to help you understand what it can do for you, the real power behind your brand.

The American Marketing Association defines a brand as the "name, term, design, symbol, or any other feature that identifies one seller's goods or service as distinct from those of other sellers." More importantly, it further defines it as the "customer experience represented by a collection of images and ideas." So what does all that mean? Simply put, your brand identity represents you. Your brand represents your reputation, your company's reputation. It tells the story of the attributes, values, purpose, strengths and passions of you and your business – who you are and what you stand for.

Your brand is one of the most valuable fixed assets your business can own. Always remember, you are your brand. It must be carefully developed to make sure that it truly represents your business, what the business is, who you are, and that it resonates with both your current customers, and those that you seek to acquire. Most important, it has to be believable. You have to be prepared to live your brand. For example, when you think of Volvo, you think well-built, comfortable, but most of all, you think safety. Why? Because they have spent decades consistently focused on quality and safety, assuring us that Volvo is a very safe car to drive. Studies prove it to be true. They live it. They stand by it.

A brand is a combination of logos, colors, words, font, personality, price and service. It can be a bundle of attributes. It is having a consistent message of who you are. It's your identity and should be the same everywhere, in everything you do, from your website, Facebook, Twitter, Google+, business cards to wherever you are putting you and your business out there. It's not just about a logo though. It's about something that people can relate to, associate with, something that resonates with them, has meaning to them and keeps them coming back to you.

Great brands are easy to recognize. Everyone knows brands like Coca Cola, Budweiser, Google, Apple, Ford, and Zappos. Companies like these spend a lot of time, money and effort to build their brands to become recognizable household names: Zappos stands for Internet shoes; Google stands for "search"; Coca Cola is the real thing; Clydesdales represent Budweiser; Ford is built Ford-tough. Most people reach for a Kleenex, not a tissue. You Xerox copies.

Companies devote a lot of energy to make the brand mean something in people's minds. You know what you are going to get with a well-branded product or service. When Wieden + Kennedy pitched "Just Do It" to Nike, it really was not about shoes. Instead of trying to build a brand based on a commodity – their shoes – Nike built their brand on striving, sweating and sacrificing to be the best. It focused on why its customers wanted their shoes, not the shoes themselves.

Many businesses do not offer a tangible product, but rather offer a service like marketing consulting, fitness training, an investment firm or a law office. It then becomes about selling you – you are your product and need to build you as the brand. It helps to establish why people want to buy from you or use your service as opposed to someone else. Names like Stanley Steemer, Terminex, Google are common household names that you think about when you need carpets cleaned, bugs exterminated or to search through consistent messaging and branding. You need to find your niche, build your reputation around providing excellent customer service and delivery, that you are who you say you are and deliver what you say you are going to. It's that simple, yet so powerful in helping your business thrive.

Many successful people use their personal brand to achieve great careers, and your personal brand in many ways is synonymous with your reputation. It refers to the way other people see you. Are you an expert? Are you a genius? Are you trustworthy? What do you stand for? What do you represent? What ideas and images pop up as soon as someone hears your name? Two powerful examples of what happens when you develop a very successful personal brand are my mentor, coach and friend, Jennifer Nicole Lee, who inspired me to write this and was gracious enough to write the forward for this book, and Yahoo's CEO Marissa Mayer.

Jennifer Nicole Lee, or JNL as she is referred to, is the best example of someone who has, in my opinion, perfected the art of personal branding and marketing. I have followed Jennifer Nicole Lee, one of the world's most accomplished Super Fitness Models, and international celebrity, for quite some time. Her career as a top fitness expert and icon began when she lost over 80 pounds after the birth of her children. Her motivational weight loss success story caught the world's attention after she gained accolades as a professional fitness competitor, holding countless titles and crowns.

JNL, according to her website **http://jennifernicolelee.com**, is the CEO and visionary powerhouse behind JNL Worldwide, Inc., Due to her successful globally broadcasted and marketed fitness and wellness products, books, digital products, e-commerce and merchandise, she is internationally recognized in over 110 different countries. JNL is a fitness celebrity, a best-selling author, a highly sought-after spokes model, being the name, face and body of all of her lifestyle brands, wellness products, exercise equipment, DVDs, home, bath, bedding, spa and electronic downloads and websites. JNL herself is her extremely successful global mega-brand.

JNL is an exemplary case study in what to do to excel in marketing and brand building, and inspires women worldwide to grow to their full potential. JNL has mastered the unlimited marketing and sales potential of the Internet, creating a vast number of e-commerce sites, and .com's that earn hefty residual income via the web. She is a bestselling author of numerous books on diet, nutrition, and exercise, and a contributor to many magazines and eBooks, such as Oxygen, Fitness Rx and Bodybuilding.com. She also runs an international consulting firm, having coached thousands of women from around the globe, including myself, and motivates many to launch and grow new businesses. She hosts weekend fitness retreats drawing women from all over the world to simply meet her and hear her speak. She is a powerful marketing expert, appearing in numerous globally broadcast infomercials for her signature products including Ab Circle, Pro, Mini Circle, and Chest Magic, and on top shopping networks, such as QVC and The Home Shopping Network. All this started with taking her weight loss story, and building a complete brand that is real and believable. She lives and breathes her personal brand. Every day she demonstrates her dedication and relentless energy to being true to her goal of helping and empowering women. (To learn more about JNL Worldwide, go to **www.jennifernicolelee.com.**)

Building a personal brand is not just about owning your own business like JNL has done. It can be about establishing yourself within a corporate environment. Consider Marissa Mayer, the woman who made Google successful and is now Yahoo's CEO, as an example of how personal brand building can positively impact a career. Mayer, who according to Fortune Magazine, is the youngest head of a Fortune 500 company. She doesn't fit the tech geek image - people with pocket protectors and thick glasses - but claims she does code all night. She didn't grow up immersed in technology, and didn't learn how to use a mouse until her freshman year at Stanford. She just happened to take a computer science class, and knew that it was what she wanted to do. After graduating from Stanford, she had 14 job offers and chose Google. She climbed the ranks from programmer to vice president. According to Mayer, she refuses to be stereotyped and put into a defined box. Mayer instead defined herself and her unique abilities. She understood other's perceptions of her, and used that information to create her personal brand. And that brand has led to great success for her.

When you begin to think about developing your own brand, either personal or for your business, the last thing you want to do is be like everyone else. Like Mayer, you don't want to be stereotyped, but you want to be unique and discernable. Your brand has to plant itself in the hearts and minds of customers and prospects. It has to be memorable. Your brand is the focus of all your marketing efforts. It needs to say something about your business, connect with your target market and be motivating in some way to drive action, and to create loyalty.

People love brands for their personality. They need to trust it. They want to trust you. You need to decide on what kind of personality you want your brand to have. You need to be true to that brand, to use it as a means to connect with your audience. Outside of your family and personal friends, people know you by your reputation, personality and your past performance. If you are a personal trainer, dentist, caterer, nutritionist, people don't know you the person. They know you by what you do and how you do it. By developing a strong personal brand, getting people to trust you, you are able to attract more potential clients, employees and decision-makers. You can influence what and how they think of you by being true to your brand.

Remember, a brand is a promise. It's who you are, what you deliver, how you achieve it, what makes you different from others promising the same thing. How you communicate those ideas to your targeted audience, the messages you project, the channels and the tools you use to communicate – are the way that you build a brand image. It strikes to the heart of the company. People buy from the brands they know and trust.

The same applies if you are building a personal brand. Every day, through every word and action, people are viewing your character, abilities and performance. How you perform and react will determine what people perceive you to be and create expectations for what you will continue to deliver and how. If you are demonstrating solid performance and abilities, you can be assured that you will be able to grow and be asked to take on new challenges and given opportunities.

It is important to note that your personal brand should not be confused with your personal image. Your personal image is the qualities that people identify with you. Your hairstyle, your sense of humor, what clothes you wear, favorite foods, physical characteristics. In order to transform your personal image into your personal brand which can then lead to business opportunities, means you need to be sure that your words, actions and performance help define how you are perceived. You need to polish your brand so that everyone you come in contact with says the same thing when they hear your name or see that you are up for a project or opportunity. When that promotion becomes available, are you considered for it because you have built that strong personal brand and reputation, or are you overlooked because you are not perceived as strong enough or qualified to take it even though you are the perfect fit.

There are many benefits to building a personal brand. As your brand becomes more established, it helps you attract the right clients, the right position, and the next promotion. As you achieve that right mix of clients, or that higher position, your income potential increases as you become viewed as an expert in your field. Once your brand is established, you will no longer be anonymous. As your name, expertise and strengths become better known, people will be drawn to you, and you will become top of mind when they start looking for someone to lead that next project, take on that next job. You stand out among the crowd as the go-to person who will effectively get the job done. A strong personal brand encourages people to put you into leadership roles, giving you more prestige, perceived value and greater recognition.

Just as you reap the benefits of building your personal brand by proving your worth, there are things that it will not do for you. It will not cover up incompetence. If you are not able to perform the job, people will pick up on that quickly, and it will be reflected in your brand image. It will not make you famous, nor should it. It takes hard work to be successful. Just because you build a brand, unless you deliver what you promise, it will not cover up if you are not qualified to do what you say you can do. Nor will just saying it help you reach your goals. You have to make sure that you set the right goals, maintain a level of excellence, actively promote your brand, and be consistent. Your personal brand is about influencing people to choose you. You must deliver on everything you say you are going to do, and do it with excellence.

Regardless of age, position or business you happen to be in, everyone needs to understand the importance of branding. You are the CEO of your own company – Me, Inc. To be in business today, your most important job is to be head marketer for the brand called YOU. Your personal brand is a powerful, concise positive idea that people think of when they think of you. It is what you stand for – your values, abilities and actions. It drives and influences how others perceive you, and gives you the chance to turn that perception into opportunity.

A personal brand allows you to influence your target market, how they perceive you and what they find valuable. To be effective, your personal brand must show that you are different, that you are new and original, rather than a follower. It must show that you are among the best in what you do. As JNL says "It's not bragging if you can back it up." If you can show that what you do is better than what anyone else is doing, you have earned the bragging rights. Part of backing it up is your ability to be authentic and sincere. Your brand must be built on truth of who you are, what your strength is, and what makes you good at what you do. You must effectively communicate this to your audience.

The web makes this more critical than ever before. Anyone can have a website. How do you know which sites are worth visiting one time or multiple times, which sites to bookmark? Branding. The sites you go back to are the sites and brands you trust. They are the sites where the brand name will tell you that the visit will be worth your time again and again. The brand is a promise of the value you'll receive.

It's a process to build a brand, to build that identity. It is not just a presentation, nor is it a marketing campaign. A good brand will deliver your message in a clear, concise manner, connect you with your customers and motivate them to visit you, and will increase your credibility. Regardless of whether it's a personal or business brand, it is not built in a day. It takes time and consistency to build a brand that people know, trust and respond to. Building a successful brand is perpetual. You have to continually evolve your brand. Look at Oprah as the perfect example of growing a brand over time with consistency, sincerity and her achievements. She didn't start that way. She was born into poverty and had a difficult adolescence. She spent years acting, doing her talk shows, and helping other women before becoming what she is today – a global media mogul. She continues to work hard, to build her empire, and is still the world's only African-American billionaire.

As long as you focus on developing a sense of purpose for what you want your brand to be, and continue to back it up over and over, you can build a successful brand. The right mix of marketing messaging will help your followers see the value of your brand, and see you as real. You can't force it. You have to define it, build it, and live it. Let it take roots and grow.

Ready to start the journey of defining, developing and living your brand? Let's get started.

Now that you know need a brand, how do you get it?

"Great products and wonderful service is not enough. To inspire brand loyalty, you need to go above and beyond traditional business tenets and start a movement your customers can't wait to be a part of"
Bayard Winthrop, Founder & CEO at American Giant

To build a brand that stands out in the crowd, especially with the Internet allowing businesses to extend beyond the local market and into the global space, you have to do more than offer the best products and service in your industry. You have to create a following that will stand by you when things go wrong, push you to be better, and seek you out above the competition. When you achieve that, you have to deliver what you say you will and to be as loyal to your customers as they are to you. It is a partnership between you and your customers.

Consumers today have more choices and more power to support companies that give them what they want. It's not just about access, convenience, or outstanding customer service anymore. These are basic requirements for brands, table stakes for you to be in your chosen business. People are now seeking brands that fit with their values and give them something to believe in – plus the best quality and price on the market.

Take for example San-Francisco based Uber Technologies, Inc., who offers online limousine and private cab booking services via mobile phones. When you think of cab services, you don't always think of a high quality experience, but that is exactly what Uber Technologies promises. According to Andrew MacDonald, general manager, they are focused on providing quality at all price points, whether using their black car service or taxi service. That's what their brand stands for. This brand promise drives everything Uber does from the look and feel of its app to the rigorous training it provides to the drivers in its network. From the very beginning, there was a lot of conversation internally around what the Uber brand looks like – from the ordering process to the receipt, to how drivers dress and how clean the car is.

Building an identity for your brand is one of the most complex, time consuming and difficult tasks, but one of the most rewarding, beneficial and important ones. You must carefully consider and spend time on it, not rush through to get to the next phase of brand building. It's important to have a strong brand name that stands for something, and that you determine what it stands for. Consumers associate different names with different things, some of which may be quite obvious and strong, like Volvo is associated with safety. If you don't define it, the market and your competitors will do it for you, and it may not be what you want.

What about if you already have a brand? If you are not seeing the success you are looking for, your brand might be a little weak and disjointed. The single biggest mistake people make is that they either brand themselves for the sake of doing it or without taking the time to define their passion, their products or services. They may not have clearly defined what they want to be to their customers. Sometimes, while time-consuming and can cost additional money, it's worth rebranding, or at least changing some element of your brand to better connect with your consumers to better convey who and what you are.

Often, naming your business is one of the toughest steps to building a brand. Many small businesses see branding as something they'll get around to when they hit a certain number of sales so they don't focus the necessary time and energy to create their image and identity from the beginning. Remember that your identity is not your image. Your identity is who you say you are. Your image is who your customers say you are. By building the right identity, you can influence the perception of your brand and in the long run create the image you want.

The common misconception is that branding is just about a name or a logo. Many people will say things like "I want a brand like Apple," but they don't really know what that means or how to make it happen. Branding doesn't have to be expensive or drawn out to be effective. Many think building a brand begins with external pieces such as brochures, websites, and business cards, but really, it should start on the inside of your company. Everyone in the company should understand what the company's brand is and how it should manifest itself every day. Taking the time to sit by yourself, and your team if you have one, and ask who are you as a company, who do you want to be and what kind of personality do you want to convey? A well-defined and executed brand will showcase your expertise and place you in a position to thrive in a highly competitive, uncertain environment.

There are five common approaches to naming either a brand or a company: names of people, animals, places or symbols, such as Ford, Johnson & Johnson and Apple. Others actually describe the business with their name such as General Motors, US Airways and General Instruments. Names can be made up or unrelated like Yahoo, Google and Zappos. They can be made from contractions, acronyms or initials such as IBM, FedEx and ESPN. And the last approach is a benefit-related name like Spic and Span, Head & Shoulders, and I Can't Believe It's Not Butter. For small businesses, the best approach, if possible, is to go the route of benefit-related. The more opportunities you take to integrate your name, position and tagline, the more brand recognition you are likely to secure.

Because of the time and effort that it takes to build a brand, naming is one step that should take the longest. Once launched, there is typically a lot of brand equity that goes into it to make changing the name an easy task further down the road.

Like what Uber Technologies has done. If you want to grow, you need to be something that people can get behind, and to do that, you need to have an image, something people think of when they think of you. You need a brand promise. Every company has a brand in one way or another, some are just more successful than others. With shoestring budgets, lean work forces and tight schedules, many businesses don't think that they have the time or money to put into branding, or are concerned that with a fast growing company, they will outgrow their brand and have to go through a re-branding process. If you've been around for a while, you've probably already developed a solid brand. People recognize your name, what you're working on, what you offer and what you're about.

A brand is not built in a day. It takes time and consistency to build your brand into something that others recognize and respond to. Brand discovery is about figuring out what you want to do, setting goals, writing down a mission, vision, a personal brand statement and a plan on how to get there. From the company brand to the product brand, branding is a critical component to a customer's purchasing decision. The best place to start building your brand is at the core of your company. You need to be very clear about the why, what, and how of what you want to do and who you want to be. Ask yourself "why are you doing this?" The "why" part is the most crucial and will influence everything that comes after it. The "how" will help you determine the manner by which the goals will be achieved. The "what" will help you work through the details to achieving your goals.

Before you begin the process of building a brand, you need to plan, to define your brand. You need to decide what your brand stands for and how you want to be perceived. This is often called your value proposition. To effectively communicate this, you need to identify and know what business you are in. When you are defining your business, think about what outcomes people can see when they use your product or service. I have always believed that what you should be talking about is how you are solving a pain point, or how you are making life better. If don't put it out there for people in a way that they can understand what they can expect when they use your product or service, they will seek out the company who can. Part of this is defining what you really do, but not just from a standpoint of job title or company name, but what customers want you to do for them. Develop a list of what your customers really want, and how you can help them achieve it. Finally, emphasize how you are really different. You need to be sure that you identify your unique strengths, compare them against your competition and match your strengths to customer values, what's important to them.

A preliminary step is to create two lists identifying your strengths, skills, areas of expertise and your values. If you find it difficult to identify your strengths objectively, ask others to tell you as they see aspects in you that you might not see or realize are a strength. Your list of values should include what is most important to you, what you stand for, the personal values you hold as important. You should have three to five values that are close to everyone's heart and should be communicated either directly or indirectly to your audience. The things that your audience sees should say "these guys get me", and will ultimately lead to building a trust relationship with them.

A very important word of caution when establishing value statements. You need to establish values that you believe in and can demonstrate. Just because it sounds good, doesn't mean that it is right for your brand or your business. Your values need to be genuine for you and ones that you can live up to, if not today, ones you are actively working to achieve. If you want to be known for customer service but you don't take or return their calls, customer service excellence is not your brand's value. Don't create values you can't deliver or that are not representative of your business just because they sound good, or you think that is what people want to hear or think you represent.

Armed with these skills and values lists, look for opportunities that reinforce your skills and values and then set your goals to convey this image. Because you're personal brand is developed from the thoughts, words and reactions of other people, it is shaped based on how you present yourself publically. It is important that you decide how you want others to see you when you build that image. There are several key questions you should ask yourself when you are setting your goals about how would you like your potential customers to think of you. What do you want them to say about you? What do you want them to think about when they think of your business? And most important, how can you publicly be that brand? This includes defining what you want to be about, the key ideas that you want people to associate with you and your business, and defining your key areas of expertise.

Every good brand is defined by what they are good at. Nike and Champion both brand themselves as expert in creating quality and fashionable sportswear, and are recognized by that distinctive swoosh and the "C" on the sleeve. The host of Top Gear, Jeremy Clarkson is an expert on cars.

If you own your business, keep in mind that your company brand should not be different than your personal brand. Who you are, who your business is should be the same. Make sure that you create a brand name that you can breathe life into and one that can be taken seriously. You don't need to sound like a company, but you do need to sound like a company that cares.

One thing you need to consider is that your personal brand has the potential to last longer than your lifetime. While your current products or the projects that you are working may no longer be available or are wrapped up, your personal brand will continue and has the potential to add value to each new product, service or project that you are involved with. If done correctly, people will follow you from project to project, product to product if they feel connected to you and has the potential to ensure that you don't have to start from scratch with every new venture. If well-defined and executed, it will showcase your expertise and put you in the position to succeed even in uncertain times. It will identify you as a high-caliber professional in your chosen field.

A brand is not something that you can just throw together all at once. You need to decide on what direction to take it, how it will evolve as you do, and test it to see if it works now and into the future. Unless you are starting out as a well-known personality, the first thing you need to do is focus on clearly stating what you do, not who you are since most people most likely will not know who you are. People care about what you do, what you are offering, so choosing the right name in the first place will help build and establish your brand recognition and recall. Think about the keywords that best describe what you do, what people will Google when they are searching for your product or service. Your name has to reflect your product in order for you to be searchable and show up.

A brand is not static. As new events, products, and services evolve, you may be required to re-establish your brand. New opportunities can be part of your brand building. Change brings opportunity and can create gaps in your vision and your strategy. Regular reviews will help you stay focused and cause you to continually keep your brand promise in the forefront. No matter how good your idea or your content is, it is important that you keep it fresh by adding new elements to your brand, new layers to what you represent.

Continue to learn and update your knowledge base. Everything is changing so fast these days. New experts, new products attempt to come out every day and will try to take your followers, and ultimately your customers, from you. What worked for you yesterday may not work tomorrow. Continue to challenge yourself to remain one who is viewed as the expert, the go to person, the product or service that everyone wants to continue to use and trust. Focus on areas where you can have something new to say or can add more value. Don't allow yourself to become stale with yesterday's knowledge. Be sure that you set yourself up to be viewed as a leading-edge expert in your chosen field.

Use social media to create this public image and style, a voice for yourself, through well-known outlets like LinkedIn, Facebook and Twitter, and to continue to evolve your brand. Develop a website that is all about you to give people a place to connect with you, to get to know you. Grow your presence through forums, blogs and groups. Be sure to include a mini-bio at the end of each post. Spend time developing your About page and use it to help people get to know you and your personal brand. People will remember only a few things about you, so it is important to focus on telling the story that best describes your brand. Use your personal story as the basis for your expertise. Your actions, well executed over time, will establish a pattern that will be associated with your name – with your brand. While this will be discussed in more detail in later chapters, how you want to do this and how you want to be perceived needs to be a part of your brand definition phase.

Once you have identified your brand identity, it's time to develop your logo. A logo is a simple representation of your brand through the use of an icon-sized image or mark. When your logo is seen by either a current or previous customer, it should convey an emotional response to your brand identity. A simple but unique logo will translate more quickly in their mind than a complex, detailed design. Think Nike or McDonald's – most of the biggest brands have very simple logos that are easy to remember and associate with the company.

When creating your logo, make sure that it will be recognizable in any size, anywhere you chose to use it, from billboards to business cards. Whether you create it yourself or hire a designer, make sure it is created in vector format, in both a colored and a black and white version. Be sure that your design looks good whether in color or printed in black and white.

Color must be considered for both your overall brand identity and your logo. Determine what color you want to have associated with your brand. Red and orange are attention-grabbers, but can be perceived as bold and brash; blue and green can make a bold splash but can also be perceived as calm. Black, brown or gray tend to be viewed as ultra-modern, professional. Stick with 2-3 colors for your brand at the most. Your target audience should be your primary thought when selecting colors, followed by your personality as different colors can portray different emotions to your customers than they do to you. Choose colors wisely to create a greater bond with your customers.

Once you have decided on color for your brand identity and logo, you now need to select a font. A font has a personality of its own so sometimes it can be a challenge to choose what goes with your brand. To maintain consistency throughout your brand identity, choose two or three fonts to use consistently with your brand. You may need a customized font for your logo and website title, a purchased font for your headings, and an easy-to-read font for body text. Keep in mind while you might like a font that is playful, modern or elegant, it is more important to choose a font that is easy to read. If the name of the company or the tagline cannot be read quickly, that font you choose will not help your brand.

After defining the elements of your brand identity, it is useful to put together brand guidelines. Brand guidelines can be as simple as a single page document that details the elements required for using your brand, your logo placement and usage. It will include what fonts are acceptable, what the pantone colors are to be used. It will describe how and when to use taglines, what minimum size both your logo and tagline needs to be. It will detail how and where a logo can be used.

This is important for web development, printing and production of your different medium and will ensure that you have a consistent brand image in all places that you are represented. Consistency will help with your brand recognition and awareness to make sure that you look and feel the same everywhere your name is used. While it may seem like a tedious exercise, you will spend less of your valuable time going back and forth with your vendors and print shops if they have a concise document to follow.

With all the individual components that make up your brand identity completed, you need to consider where your brand will be displayed to your audience. This includes everything from business cards, stationary, website, brochures, signage and social media accounts. Each of these elements should have a consistent brand design appearance so that customers will recognize you anywhere, from a business card to your website, to a search engine.

Once you have completed all these tasks, you now have the foundation for your brand identity for which you are now ready to start to build the voice of your brand.

Why You? What makes you special?

*"We believe people with passion can change the world for the bet-
ter... and that those people who are crazy enough to think they
can change the world, are the ones who actually do."*
Steve Jobs, co-founder, chairman, and CEO of Apple Inc.

Through branding yourself or your company, you are communicating
a clear message of who you are and what you want to be known for. It's
not enough to be known for what we do in these highly competitive
times. We must be known for what we do differently. People need to
know and trust that you are the best solution to their problem, that
you offer the best product for their hard-earned money. To do this,
you need to find new ways to describe who you are and what you do.
Define what makes you special, different, unique from anyone else
out there. How you stand out in the clutter of offerings available. This
becomes the voice of your brand.

Today, consumers are flooded with products, services, offers,
media and messages. Industries such as airlines, banking, and retail
are all challenged with essentially offering the same service, product
and core offering. Some companies, such as Charles Schwab, have
earned increased market share with innovative offerings, but generally
the only differentiator for these industries is the experience they give
their customers. It's their brand values, what they hold as operating
principles that can distinguish them from their competition. It's the
"how" you do what you do, as opposed to the "what" you do.

It's not about job titles, positions, job descriptions. It's about defining what you do that adds outstanding, distinguished, distinctive and measurable value. Telling the story of what you are most proud of, what you have accomplished, and making it relevant to those you are communicating your brand to. If you are trying to build a personal brand, you need to constantly ask yourself:

- What am I most passionate about?
- What am I really good at?
- What do I want others to know about me and how can it be of use to them?
- How can I add value?
- What experience do I have?
- What makes me most proud?
- What special skills and knowledge do I have?
- What makes me different than anyone else, especially those in my space?
- What do I want to be known for?

A strong voice means your audience will recognize you no matter where they see you. Your website copy, marketing materials, blogs and social media sites, your brand should have a consistent tone that is recognizable to customers. The visual impact of your brand identity is built one element on top of the other. Key is to remain consistent and relevant to your audience.

What makes you stand out in a crowd? You don't necessarily need to be, for example, the best fitness trainer out there. Things like always being dependable, supportive and reliable, offering to help out and make a contribution, being well prepared, anticipating and solving problems, finding creative ways to save money or reduce waste, coming up with innovative ideas and showing that they work, completing projects on time and within budget, making contact with people and keeping in touch or promoting others and referring people to each other are elements that go into building a strong brand identity. Many are skilled in your field, but if you demonstrate that you go beyond just a certain skill set, that you do it with integrity and dependability, you will grow your brand credibility. It will define you as someone special in your field and others will seek you out from your competitors.

Your brand needs to be something that is unique and valuable to you. You need to convey that you are something real, something different. Basically, what differentiates you from your competition. It's how you describe yourself and your business that can make you sound like everyone else. Don't define yourself by what you do. Start defining yourself as a noun. The way we describe ourselves is critical to making a good first impression.

Unique selling proposition is a term marketers' use and one that you need to think about when you are creating your brand and how to establish a good first impression. A unique selling proposition (USP) is just what the term implies – what makes your business unique and attractive to the consumer. What differentiates you from your competition? USPs are a great way to sell your product or service. Your USPs are the major contributors to what makes your business successful and should be the basis for your brand strategy. Most brands concentrate on several of the most powerful and easily communicated proposition benefits to create a clearly understood brand message. Consider these examples:

Avis. We're number two. We try harder.

This USP does a great job of turning a drawback into a benefit. For a long time, Avis was the second-largest car rental company, after Hertz. In fact, Avis was struggling just to stay afloat. As part of a total image makeover, Avis hired the ad agency Doyle Dane Bernbach to develop a new ad campaign. The campaign was so successful, Avis' market share went from 11% to 35% in just four years.

M&M's. The milk chocolate melts in your mouth, not in your hand.

This is an example of how even a rather off-beat USP can be catchy and compelling. Through using the idea of making a selling point out of the fact that your product doesn't melt if you hold it, M&Ms created a very successful brand image for themselves.

Other good examples include:

- **Anacin** "Fast, fast, incredibly fast relief".

- **Domino's Pizza:** "You get fresh, hot pizza delivered to your door in 30 minutes or less—or it's free."

- **FedEx:** "When your package absolutely, positively has to get there overnight."

- **Metropolitan Life:** "Get Met. It Pays."

Unique selling propositions are why customers are buying your products and services, forming the basis for your brand values, forming an alliance with brand loyalty. They are not static and should evolve as market conditions change, and should always reflect your forward-looking business strategy. Once you define your values, it's important to make sure that your customers' experience reflects these values in every aspect of doing business with you. This means that you need to tailor every marketing message, every element to project your brand values, from the staff that you use, the products you produce, the messages on your advertising, and even the way you handle complaints. Building a respected brand takes a lot of hard work and a commitment from everyone involved to make it happen.

The way we describe ourselves is critical to making a good first impression. Companies spend a great deal of money on packaging their goods and services. Marketer Seth Godin refers to this as knowing your super power. According to Godin, everyone in the "justice league" has their own unique role. It was who they are and how they are valuable to the people around them. When defining your brand, you need to find your super power. Things to include in that first impression for a personal brand include your name, portrait, bio, vision, personal style, pitch, business card and social media sites. For your business, this translates to your business name, logo, profile, values, professional image, presentation, flyers and website.

The three pillars of a good brand are authenticity, consistency and clarity. These will serve as the basis for everything that connects people to you, both logically and emotionally. People need to know about you, about the work that you do. They want to meet you, talk with you, and experience you. To do this, you need to be very visible and create a high online presence through either the development of your own or regular contribution to a blog.

If you don't want to commit to the time to creating and growing your own blog, you can still create a credible, brand following. Comment on others blogs, post to others blogs, post useful links and information, and write reviews on books, products and services. Have a presence by attending networking meetings and events, connect with people and keep in touch, get involved with organizations and groups in your field, and in the areas that you want to target, deliver talks and presentations, volunteer to be a guest speaker, write articles and case studies, promote local events and activities of interest. Through all these, be prepared to tell your unique story. Use them to reflect your brand favorably. They are a great way to get to know people who could become followers and ultimately customers.

What do you want people to know about you?

> *"Above all else, be yourself – be genuine – and you'll find success no matter what you do."*
> Chris Pirillo, Internet Personality and founder of Gnomedex

Everyone has a personal image. It's the collection of qualities people identify with you – your sense of humor, hairstyle, clothing, favorite food, physical characteristics. These things make up the image that people think of when they think of you. Your personal brand is different, because it is how other people perceive you. In the best circumstance, a personal image is an accurate reflection of the personal brand you are trying to convey. Mother Theresa looked like a woman dedicated to lifelong servitude of the poor and indigent, and she is perceived as the modern-day saint. There is complete integrity between her personal image and personal brand.

You have been creating a personal brand without even realizing it. So rather than letting others define it for you, take control and transform that personal image into a personal brand that creates business opportunities. To do this, you need to define how you want prospective customers, colleagues and peers to see you. It's packaging the things that make you great at what you do, and sending that message out to the world. People work with you not because of your size or reach, but because they know you, your reputation, and your character. You create value for yourself in everything you do.

While there is no definitive template to follow when it comes to creating your brand, there are three key considerations that will help you succeed. The first is simplicity. When developing your brand, keep it simple and focused on what you do, not on impressing others. Keep it clean. We've all heard of KISS – keep it simple silly (ok, I improvised). Same holds true when you are developing what you want people to know about you, how you want them to describe you.

Second, you need to consider longevity of where you are today and where you ultimately want to end. Once you've decided what you want your focus to be, hold true to that. You won't see results immediately. Give it time to gain exposure and recognition. It took Nike 15 years to gain the brand recognition of their swoosh and their tagline "Just Do It."

The final is consistency. Once you have determined what you what people to know about you, be sure that you have a consist message in all your mediums. Everything you say, every ad, every message, should have the same look and feel, especially important when you are just starting out creating a brand name for yourself. If you are constantly changing what you say, what you look like, including what colors and fonts you use, you will not get the brand recognition you need to start to build a steady brand.

In creating your brand, it is important that you focus on your prospects. These are potential customers that you want to attract to your website, your Facebook, Twitter, and ultimately, your products and services. At this point, you need to define your ideal customer in detail and create your brand with this ideal customer in mind. Research who you think will buy your products and services, their likes and dislikes, their lifestyle and needs. If you are already selling your product or service, look at your current customer base. Define what they look like as a starting point. This is known as your target market.

Since most businesses cannot take on every segment of the market, you need to find your niche market – those potential customers most likely to buy the products and services you are selling. While this could be as simple as a demographic group, you need to think beyond just demographics and look at values. What things does your potential customer value? What do they believe in? Where and how do they spend their time? The clearer you are identifying your target market, the more defined your messaging can be, allowing you to connect deeper with your potential customers. One of the most important things you can do when creating your brand is to become very clear on the qualities and attributes of your ideal customer and target market. Once you have defined your primary target market, you can identify who might be your secondary and tertiary, but your main focus should always be how you grow your primary market since that is your greatest opportunity.

This will allow you to focus on the core message for your brand. Define some of your biggest challenges and lessons in life. Describe what types of things you have overcome and learned to gain your knowledge and expertise, and what you want to use from this to teach others. This will help you come up with the compelling reasons why potential customers should do business with you over any of your competitors. You should be able to communicate to your target market what sets you apart in your market. If you can't answer this question, you are losing a critical concept of branding: how to differentiate yourself.

You should always know who your key competitors are and what they are doing. This is something that you should do on an ongoing basis. You should know your competition's business as well as they know their business, as well as you know your own. It is important that you have a good understanding of how they are addressing your primary target market. While it is easier to do in a mature market with one or two well-entrenched competitors, you should continually be aware of what they are doing, not that you want to do the same but to find your competitive advantage.

Think about what differentiates you from your competition. Differentiation helps you stand out. When you clearly define what unique capabilities and values you bring to your customer base, and describe what gaps you fill, it becomes the basis for your unique selling proposition. Remember, a unique selling proposition (USP) is defined as what makes your business unique and attractive to the consumer. It defines what differentiates you from your competition. They are a great way to sell your product, and serve as the major competitive advantage.

In several sections of this book, I have focused on defining the core values of your business. Core values are things that you share with your target market. It is very critical that you write these down and effectively communicate them as this is what connects you to your target market on an emotional level. Along with what differentiates you from your competition, consider what your customers expect from you on a consistent basis. This is known as your brand promise, the expectations that the customer has about your company. A brand promise determines what you are passionate about. When you combine that passion with the needs of your target market, your brand promise becomes the anchor for what you are delivering. It is the essence of the company and includes its voice, image, personality and greatest strengths. It is the delivery of the brand.

An example of a brand promise is that if a research company brands itself as a fast provider of reliable information, the brand has promised its customers that it will deliver accurate, usable data in a defined timeframe, and that team will provide comprehensive reports in a timely manner. If the company doesn't deliver, it has broken its brand promise and stands to lose that customer forever. And it won't be just that customer. As much as word of mouth can help you grow your business, it can just as easily destroy it. Be very cautious in how you define yourself and make sure that you are able to deliver on that promise.

For those adopting the concept of brand promise, many of them focus on developing a brand that attracts attention and sets them apart in their brand's space. To ensure that you deliver on your brand promise, you must efficiently organize all aspects of your business to meet that promise. Without it, you could easily break your promise.

This needs to flow through every aspect of your business in order for consumers to believe what you are promising. Without it, you risk losing credibility. Customers may not know what goes on behind the scenes in delivering your product or service, but how it is handled could have an impact on your brand promise. If you promise fast delivery but you are not able to deliver in a timely manner, you will not have delivered on your promise of fast delivery. If you have sales or customer service resources, be sure that they are trained and knowledgeable in your products. When they are able to sufficiently answer questions immediately, productivity and customer trust increases. While it may sound hokey, be sure that they smile when talking with customers. In a call center that I managed, I ordered mirrors for everyone that we placed on the side of their terminals. While they didn't necessarily like it, our customer satisfaction scores for that team improved when they were able to visibly see themselves talking to customers.

From your brand promise stems your brand personality. This will define what style you deliver your brand promise. Do you want to be dependable but surprisingly fun? Will you be the hero, with better-than-the-rest deals that don't compromise on quality? With your ideal customer in mind, make sure that your brand personality will appeal to your target market. This may mean toning down a playful branding scheme to create a neutral brand that will have appeal to a wider audience.

Positioning is the way that consumers think about your brand. It is their emotions and perceptions about your brand, your image. There are two key parts to the positioning statement. The positioning promise is the benefit you promise consumers, and the reason why they should believe you can deliver on that promise. An effective positioning statement should be focused on a single idea. It should be memorable. It should be written so that it is true, accurate and precise, clearly defining the benefits to the consumer, and it must be believable in order to give credibility to your brand. It does need to be competitive and unique, a way for you to stand out in the crowd, and make consumers want to choose you. Finally, it must be substantive, relevant and important to those who you want to buy from you.

There are four steps to developing a good positioning statement. First, you need to understand who your target audience is. You need to be as specific and narrow as possible to develop that picture. Things to consider are: does it matter where they are located geographically, their lifestyle characteristics, their product usage, industry or demographically by age, sex, income, education. It is important to understand your audience so you can speak directly to their needs and use words that they are most likely to relate to. If you already have customers, take a look at their make-up and target those areas that they have in common as your core to developing your positioning statement.

Second, you need to decide what is the most important benefit that you offer to your target audience. If you already have a customer base, find out why they chose and stay with you. When you develop your brand position, it is important to find an objective source of input. Ask questions of your current customers to gain a better understanding so that you can apply it to a broader audience and extend your reach.

The third step is to decide what type of benefit you can deliver. There are three types of these statements to consider. The first, benefit positioning, identifies the basic positioning, for example, "Nobody

beats Federal Express when it comes to reliable overnight delivery."
End-benefit positioning is the second type that delivers an emotional
payoff from that basic statement. "You don't have to worry about your
package arriving on time if you use Federal Express." is meaningful
and valuable. The third type is the end-end-benefit, those that directly
reflect on the consumer. "FedEx. When it absolutely, positively has to
be there overnight."

Finally, when you have written what you think is the right positioning statement, test it against the checklist – is it memorable, substantive, relevant, important, true, accurate, precise and clearly defines the
benefits to the consumer. If you feel that it does, you are ready to put
it all together and launch your business.

When defining your brand personality, you need to consider the
aspects of your work that a potential customer will find of most value
when they hire you. At the core of your brand identity is to project the
personality, the means by which you communicate what you deliver to
your customer base. One way to do this is through the use of a tagline.
A tagline can be used with your logo. Sometimes referred to as a slo-
gan, a tagline allows you to say a little more about your brand that the
logo can by itself. It is a short phrase or statement that is tied to and
associated with your business's brand name and/or one of your products. The primary purpose is to add depth to the brand identity and
can be either functional or emotional. Certain colors will be better at
portraying your image that others.

Most of the time, taglines take on a different role depending on
your naming approach. When using a benefit-driven tagline, it should
appeal to the emotional side of the consumer. It should enhance
the positioning benefit, not confuse with a different message. A non-
benefit tagline should state the benefit in a way that the consumer
understands and is able to remember it. Some power brands, like
Charmin, are able to use their brand in their tagline. When you see
the tagline "Please don't squeeze the Charmin", you can't say the

tagline without using the product name. Or what about Bounty – the quicker picker-upper. While this doesn't work for all brands, it can be a powerful way to join your product name and tagline to make it far more recognizable.

Procter & Gamble is a branding powerhouse in integrating product names and taglines, as well as bringing that emotional element into it. Not only did they include the Jif brand name in its tagline, it plants the thought that the quality is superior when they say that "Choosy moms chose Jif". Crest's "Look Ma, no cavities".

When you are developing your tagline, there are some guidelines to keep in mind. A tagline should not be more than nine words, the fewer the better so that it can be remembered. It should be meaningful. While cute and catchy is fun, you want people to think about the idea behind your product or service. Choose words that paint a picture, that grab people and are easy to remember. The goal of creating a tagline is to communicate or enhance the brand position, not just to entertain or amuse the consumer. If you can, include your brand name in your tagline.

Some good examples include: American Express – Don't leave home without it. AT&T – Reach out and touch someone. General Electric – We bring good things to life.

You may need a brand story to more accurately define your business. A brand story is simply the "About Us" of a company, and the core concept that every business rotates around. Starbucks uses their brand story to create an atmosphere present in every item in the public eye, from the actual cafes to the products sold in retail stores. Your brand story can be about you, where you came from, your personality, your goals, your mission, your values, and definitely your passions. If you are struggling to get a clear picture of what your brand should look like, write out your story and it may help you better develop that picture.

The more time that you spend on this part of the brand building process upfront, the more likely people will be able to identify with you, connect with your brand, and the more success you will have in the long run as you start the process of launching your business.

Use Your Brand to Create Relationships

*We used to put the brand in the middle. Now the consumer
is smack-dab in the middle of everything we do. And that
means we need to understand who our customer is.*
— *Joaquin Hidalgo, Brand Chief Marketing Officer, Nike*

Emerging technologies have significantly changed the way customers interact with you, think about you, relate to you and compare you to others like you. Think about your own buying habits, and how you research what you are looking for before you leave home when buying big ticket items. Buyers have looked at reviews, your website, compared not just your products but your customer service, your hours and location, your service guarantees to learn more about you before ever contacting you. Buying online allows them to easily compare and buy from whom they perceive to be the best price value.

These technologies are forcing brands to re-evaluate how they go to market, how they represent themselves. Your brand is more than what you say it is. It's not only about the products and services you offer, but it's also the experiences you create. In order to differentiate and build stronger, deeper relationships with customers, brands must now design their own unique interactions and experiences.

As stated in previous chapters, brands are built on a brand promise. Consumers are aware of the value of their interactions with you and the power this gives them in helping you achieve your success. They must see that you give them real value through tactics like content marketing and "freemium" models in exchange for their attention and ultimately their data. You want to be able to build a database of prospects that you can market to and to do this, requires that they see the value you offer and trust you enough to give you their information. Bottom line, you need to give in order to receive.

With every interaction, you need to think about the consumer. What impression are you leaving with those interactions? You should try to build relationships with as many people as possible. When you know their names and details about them, it will leave a strong impression that you are as interested in them as they are in you, and will encourage them to talk about you to others.

While Facebook is a great place to gain exposure and to build strong personal relationships with your target market and with people that you know, it is important that you use it to build your personal brand. Make it clear to your followers who you are and what you represent. One way to achieve this is to complete your profile with interesting and relevant information, not just random facts. Be sure to use the specific privacy settings to protect your more personal information. Block your public profile and sort your friends in lists so that you show different parts of who you are to your different audiences.

Once you have your Facebook profile in order, do the same with your other social tools. Look at your Google+, Windows Live, Yahoo!, and other profiles, and implement your personal brand there as well. Be sure to include a professional photo and links back to your other sites. Use LinkedIn as a personal online resume to talk about your experience, and to help your followers understand your background and give credibility to what you are offering. Create a Twitter account, a form of micro conversations, and begin to blog as next steps.

Blogging, if done consistently, can be used as a compliment to your brand-building strategy. While you might think that it is different than running display ads or sharing on social media sites, it can further enhance your efforts by giving you the opportunity to demonstrate your expertise and build your credibility. Remember branding is about changing attitudes and perceptions, and allows you the opportunity to differentiate yourself from your competition. Your blog gives you the chance to accomplish this. To write an effective blog, it should have keywords that help attract your target audience search traffic to your post. It needs to have content that improves and enhances the attitudes and perceptions about your brand when people read it. Your target audience – both customers and prospects – need to see you as an expert in order to have the confidence and trust to work with you. You can do this either on your own or by also including guest bloggers to blog for, and about you. This increases your exposure by giving their followers the opportunity to discover and learn more about you.

While there are quite a few options available to build your online brand, you should just choose a few and do them really well instead of trying to do all of them ineffectively. If you don't want to spend time responding to tweets and emails, don't make it part of your brand strategy so people don't expect differently. If you only have time to answer a few emails, mention this with apologies on your Contact Us page so that they are not expecting a response, or tell them what time frame that they can expect a response. Be upfront and set expectations. The fastest way to tear down all your brand building efforts is to disappoint your audience. If you are clear with them, they will know what to expect and won't be disappointed.

Focus on building relationships with influencers, those individuals or groups who have relationships already with your target audience as they can help you build brand awareness. There are a number of ways that you can do this and seem sincere in building a relationship with them. You can comment on their writing, using their blogs to guest-post. Not only will this help you build a relationship, they will see the value in your expertise, ask your opinion and input, which further leads to your credibility, and helps to build your reputation. You can leverage them to not only learn from them, but to gain testimonials when you launch your product, to tweet your links to their followers, and to get them to share their best opportunities with you. Just be careful to not ask for more than you can give in return. It doesn't happen overnight, and is a long process to build those relationships.

What happens when a customer has a bad experience with you or you didn't deliver what you promised? You can use this to your advantage to show your customer service skills and to tell others how you turned their experience around, winning them over. A bad experience turned amazing can be more valuable than one that is expected because that customer will have interacted with you in a way beyond the normal experience. Proving that you stand true to your word and deliver what you say, make good when you don't, gives you a strong testimonial to your brand and should be leveraged to help communicate to others the value and integrity of your brand.

Remember the old adage, people will tell other people about a bad experience, but won't say anything when you deliver on time and in the expected manner. But, when something goes wrong, and you go out of your way to make it right, they will tell their friends about that experience. They will start out with telling about the bad, but will tell how you made good on your promise.

You could also take a proactive approach to customer service by spending quality time upfront, showing that customer that you really care about them, about what they want, by finding exactly what they're looking for. With the pace everyone keeps today, if you are willing to spend a few extra minutes establishing a relationship with your customers, they'll tell others. They'll tweet about your customer service and Instagram your product or service they bought from you. Done right, these can become very viral and the word about you, your products, and your customer service can spread very quickly. You do need to be prepared in the event that rapid growth does occur and have a strategy on how you are going to grow and deal with that.

Making customers feel special and heard makes them feel important, and impresses them. This leads to brand affinity. Brand affinities create word-of-mouth buzz. Become that new business that people tell others that they have to try. Especially in your early days as a start-up, marketing budgets are typically very lean. Word of mouth should be a major driver of your new customer base. Think about what can do you to get customers talking about the experience they have had with you so that you can grow your base quickly. How do you surprise and delight customers, at a minimal cost, to generate positive word of mouth. With access to all the social media tools, communication becomes key in telling your story.

No matter what your product or service you are offering, the importance of face-to-face networking still exists. You should not go into this thinking that you are going to sell or generate leads from every one of these, but use these as an opportunity to meet and engage with prospective buyers, letting them see who you are, what you are passionate about, what you represent. Evaluate what industry events make the most sense for you to spend your time for meeting prospects, to establish a genuine connection and begin to build those relationships.

These networking and social events are your opportunity to showcase you as the first introduction to your brand. Even if the person you are meeting is not in the market for what you are offering, they may be at a later time, or they may know someone who is. They can introduce you to people in their networks, thereby expanding yours. While it can be difficult, it is important that you step out of your comfort zone and interact with as many people as you can. Hand out your business card, exchange contact information. Many, myself included, not only hand out business cards, but there is value in creating a postcard-sized piece that you can hand out that gives them a little more detail about what you are offering, where they can find out more about you. Use it as a means to introduce as many people as you can to who you are and what you can do for them, how you can help with their pain points or how you can help them grow their business. This card should be about what you can do for them, not just a piece about how amazing your business is.

In order to be successful and grow, you need to establish as many relationships as you can, both online through social media and your website, and in-person. Word of mouth and referrals are key to your success unless you are a major corporation with a big budget who can use mass media including radio and television. Like Kit tells Julia Roberts in Pretty Woman., "Work it." Get out of your comfort zone and make yourself very visible. Leverage all resources available to you, partner where you can, create blogs and followers. Create a movement where you can get people to believe in you and your products, ensuring your business success.

Building Your Brand Toolkit

"Today's tools make it easier to create, manage, and manipulate a personal brand—and society has realized the value of strong, personal brands."
Frank Gruber Sr., Product Manager, AOL

For most branding campaigns, the first step is visibility. If you're General Motors, Ford or Toyota, that usually means a full flight of TV, radio and print ads designed to get billions of impressions for their brand in front of the consuming public. For your business, you have the same need for visibility, but you probably don't have the budget to buy it. That doesn't mean that you won't create brand awareness and recognition. You'll just have to work it differently.

Your first order should be the development of your brand toolkit. Your brand toolkit should contain all the marketing material you develop for your business both online and off. You need to decide which elements you feel will best help grow your brand and your business. Some are requirements just to operate a business while others you might not need immediately but should plan for when it makes sense to add for your business

There are basic elements that build the foundation for your toolkit – your business name or personal brand and your logo. Your logo is what will differentiate you and needs to be clear, memorable and legible. You want people to recognize your brand so your logo should leave an impression. Keep it simple, clean and clear. Part of this will be determining what colors and font you want to use. The colors need to be embedded in your identity. You should be sure to research or work with a designer to pick the right colors for the look and the identity you want to create. As with color, you need to determine what typography you want to use. The font you pick can convey a certain message – serifs are more formal, san serifs are more modern. Specific fonts will give a different impression. Be sure to keep it readable and avoid decorative formats.

The first thing you need in your brand toolkit are business cards. Your business card should include your logo, your preferred contact information, and if space allows, a picture of you and your brand statement or tagline. There are quite a few tools out there that will help you create your own business cards. You should be sure to always have a supply of business cards with you everywhere you go as there are always opportunities to meet potential clients or someone who knows someone looking for what you offer. Your business cards are your identity card, the "driver's license" for your business.

There should not be a business today, especially a new business that does not have a website, no matter how simple your site is. This is now a very important tool in your toolkit. When launching a site, it does not have to be complex or be layers deep. It can be as simple as an overview of your company and your product offerings, your bio, experience, and why they should do business with you, how to order your products and services. If you have a brick-and-mortar location, where is it and the hours of operation.

To help build your brand, you need to build a visually attractive site and does require putting some money into it, even if you build it yourself using tools like WordPress, a free web-based template system used to build and maintain a website or blog. The first thing you will need to set up and purchase a domain name, your web address through a service like GoDaddy or **NameCheap.com**.

Your website should be welcoming and easy to navigate. Things to consider when building your site is what you want your site visitors to think about you and your business when they come to your site. What is your main message so if they don't go past your home page, what you want them to leave the site knowing about you? Consider what color schemes you will use, what images best represent you and your brand. A good investment is professional photographs, crisp images of you even if you only use on your About Us/Bio page. It is recommended that you work with a designer to create the look and feel for your website. A good designer will help you figure out what information should and should not be included, best placement and layout. While this may cost you a bit, this is your brand image that you are portraying, how you want to be perceived. With the right images and language, you can appear larger than you really are and seem like a more viable business.

Also on your website, if you blog, there should be a place for your blogs to be posted on your site. Those who blog have a strong asset on their website than those who don't because blogs rank higher in search engines and lend more expertise to your business.

The final step is to secure a hosting account for your website. Your web designer can help you to this as well as set up your site. Most domain name services offer hosting when you purchase your domain name. Webhosting is the means by which you put your website online for all to see. Until it is hosted, no one can type **www.yourbusiness.com** and see the website you have created. In order to do this, you need to pay a webhosting company to host your website on one of their servers and take it live for all to see. Webhosting packages can run from $10/month for a starter package and can be upgraded as you need more bandwidth. A business that does everything over the web might consider a higher package on a dedicated server which means that you won't be sharing server space with any other website. These packages can start at $50 and higher depending on how much bandwidth you need. Your web designer should help guide you on how much bandwidth you need to effectively manage your website.

A significant, though often overlooked, tool in your toolkit is your email address. Your email address gives you a great opportunity to present your brand. Your email is used everywhere, from your business cards, notifications from social networks, to how best to contact you. While you can use an address like **businessname@gmail.com** from a free provider like Google, it is best to get a vanity email. A vanity email address is your business name as the domain, so it would be **yourname@yourbusiness.com**. If you own a domain name, you can configure a free email address to be associated with your domain and is of public record instead of using Gmail or another free email service provider. For example, I use **BrandMe@debbiecummings.com**, which routes to my Yahoo account.

Using a vanity email builds trust because it is associated with a domain making it virtually impossible to authenticate your identity. A vanity email is easy to remember since you can create a personalized email address that people recognize and can easily recall. It shows you are serious about your business as it does take more effort to set up than a free email and shows your attention to details. This is one of the most important investments that you can make in your business, and one that will cost the least. It can run anywhere from $12-$15 to register a domain name, and includes your vanity email address.

It is very simple to set up a vanity email. When you register your domain name (**www.yourbusinessname.com**) and find a host for your website, you can set up your email at the same time. Your email address will be available to use immediately, even if your website is not quite ready to be launched. You can check your email on your domain's registrar's website, or you can configure an email client like Outlook to send and receive emails using your new business email address.

The next item in your toolkit should be your reference sheet, or data sheet. It can be as simple as a postcard, a tri-fold brochure or full-size sheet. Your datasheet should include, at the minimum, an overview of your business, your offerings, how to contact you. It should include your picture, pictures of your products if applicable, or if you are offering a service, pictures of you engaging with your customers. If you are a personal trainer, it can be pictures of you training a client. If you are offering coaching sessions, it can be you and a client in a comfortable setting, engaged in a conversation. Talk about your successes, what differentiates your offering from your competition. It would be ideal to have testimonials or quotes from customers who have either bought or used your service and were pleased with what you offered or did for them. While you want to put this content on your website, you should create a downloadable pdf that can be printed or forwarded and shared. Think of this as your resume for your business.

For businesses offering some type of creative services, the creation of a portfolio is a very important toolkit element to showcase the work you've done in the past. This will help convince someone of your ability to accomplish the same results for them as you have for someone else. This should be prominently featured on your website. In addition to being featured on your website, you should have both a CD and print portfolio developed. There are social networks that exist that will allow you to show your creative skills and to possibly gain new clients like fig-dig.com and carbonmade.com. While you want to be sure to showcase your best work, be sure to show variety in what you have done so that you don't become locked into a certain category of service provider.

A key site to build your credibility and to establish yourself with professionals both in your chosen field and in those that you want to target is LinkedIn. LinkedIn is a social network for people in professional occupations, a powerful tool for you to make new business connections and an outlet to help expand your social media presence. One purpose of the site is to allow you to maintain a list of contact details of people with whom you have some type of relationship, called

Connections. These connections can be used as ways to build your business, and expand your brand. LinkedIn allows you to build a network of direct connections, the connections of each of their connections (second-degree connections) and their connections (third-degree connections). These second and third degree connections can be used to get an introduction to someone through a mutual contact.

Your LinkedIn profile is a combination of resume, cover letter, references and recommendations. LinkedIn allows you to either upload or design your own profile to showcase your work and community experiences. It can be used to find jobs, people, and business opportunities recommended by someone in the contact network. You can use it to create your own personal advertising, to search for new jobs, or to meet new people.

A word of caution when using LinkedIn to grow your network. While you can invite anyone to become a connection, if too many of those invites are responded to with "I don't know" or "Spam", your account may be restricted or closed.

An important feature of LinkedIn that you should fully use to help grow your brand is the LinkedIn Groups, which allow you to start or join a conversation with other LinkedIn members on a specific topic. These conversations allow you to build thought leadership, share expertise, market your brand and grow your network. In order to do this, you should look for Groups in your industry and like-minded business leaders. By interacting in groups that relate to your business, you can create an opportunity to show others you're passionate about what you do, provide valuable insight that relates to a topic that already exists by commenting, and by sharing industry insights and discussing market-specific trends. This will enable you to position yourself as a thought-leader within the group, and in turn make your business an industry leader. The more you back up your thoughts with quality content, the more the community will support you and respect you as an expert in your field. Be sure that you review the existing discussions first to better understand the best way to engage within the community. Before you start your own discussion, check to see if the discussion has already been brought up. Find ways to share information about products and services that relate to the topic.

While there are a number of benefits for both you and your business in participating in LinkedIn Groups, it does take time to nurture those relationships, for the members to learn more about you, your expertise and your business. Industry-specific groups can be a great place to look for sales opportunities, nurture leads by providing in-depth information, and close business deals.

One of the biggest opportunities to grow your online business is Facebook. With over a billion people on Facebook, it is the prime location to connect with and interact with your customers and your prospects, but so is your competition. Determine how you can develop a strategy that sets you apart from the pack so that you can effectively use this medium to grow your brand; and ultimately, your business.

When considering using Facebook, there are a few things that you should keep in mind. First, you need to decide on the objectives and goals of creating a Facebook page before you start. One thing it should not be is your company's website, but it should provide information about what you are trying to sell. Be sure to give yourself the flexibility to grow and change as Facebook develops new applications, tools and features. Think about how your brand is featured as a result of using these new tools. Just because you have accumulated over 25,000 likes and you have strategically updated your page does not mean that you have successfully marketed your product through Facebook. Evaluate how engaged your followers are by looking at how they are interacting with your daily posts, commenting and providing feedback, or have they blocked you from their newsfeed. Ask yourself if you are as engaged as they are. By using the valuable information made available by Facebook, you can learn to use it to successfully grow your brand and ultimately your business.

The first thing you need to do is to build your Facebook page and get the word out that you are there. Invite those who you think would be most likely to like you, and who would share your posts to help gain a greater following. Once your page has accumulated at least 30 likes, you will receive access to analytical information through the Facebook Insights feature. The feature tells page managers how many likes the page received during a specific time, or how many people have seen or clicked on a link posted on the page. Insights provides demographic information of the page's visitors. Because of this, the majority of your activity should be geared toward customer engagement.

A number of options are available to do this, and Facebook has applications to drive this activity. Contests allow you to quickly build a following. When considering a contest, be sure to set goals on what you are trying to achieve. A contest will enable you to build brand awareness, highlight a new product, gather feedback or even just increase the number of likes on your page. It is important that you decide what you want to measure before you put up the contest so you can measure whether it worked or not. Be reasonable. Don't think that you are going to gain 100,000 likes from one contest as that is the exception rather than the rule. If you successfully achieve your goal, think about the next goal, and set up your efforts to get you there. If you did not achieve your goal with this contest, evaluate what you could do differently and try it again. The wonderful thing about online marketing is the ability to test different messages, different means to gain your objective, and it's easy to measure and change. Carefully monitor what is going on, and always be prepared to tweak or completely change what you are doing to increase effectiveness and responsiveness.

Contests do have to be run through Facebook-approved applications. The most popular is Wildfire, powered by Google. Wildfire controls entry forms and promotions for the contest and will regulate advertisements and surveys.

Facebook has added Graph Search which returns results based on the people, maps, images and social activities within a person's social network. If someone has "liked" or "tagged" a favorite restaurant, the result would instantly show in a search for "restaurants my friends have been to." This feature will enable you to target your advertising by combining ads with search results. A person searching for 'friends who like photography" might be served with an ad for Panasonic cameras.

When using Facebook to grow your business, you need to be sure that you are frequently updating and responding immediately to comments and questions by your followers in order to build a relationship between you and your audience. Most people expect a response within 30 minutes of posting. Remember to use complaints to your advantage as they give you the opportunity to react quickly, and people will be watching to see how you respond to it. If you ignore it, they think that you have poor customer service.

In Facebook's third-quarter earnings statement, it was reported that Facebook had 12.8 million business pages as of the end of September 2012, but that only 3.5 million of those businesses post weekly. Facebook executives claim that it's because businesses get frustrated and end up with what they have termed "social media fatigue". Companies may not have seen the results that they had hoped for or were overwhelmed with all the features and options, and keeping up with the communication required to successfully run a social media strategy. It takes about six months before you see any real results. Be sure to set your expectations accordingly, and remember that Facebook is a communications tool, not a stand-alone marketing strategy.

Another tool in your brand toolkit to consider would be Twitter. Your Twitter profile should be an extension of both your Facebook and LinkedIn profiles. You need to use a distinct background and be sure to fill out your profile with a link to either your blog or your

LinkedIn profile. Many use Twitter as a way to post news updates, create brand awareness, build a wider audience and promote products and new details.

Many use Twitter tactically to increase their business by pushing products and promotions without thinking through their strategy before starting to use the tool. The first thing to consider is how you build your targeted audience. It's not just about having followers for the sake of volume, but consider who those followers are and whether they can add value to your brand. Think about who you want in your target audience so that you can get a return on your time and energy investment. Evaluate your products and services, and then search Twitter for potential followers who could become customers or potential partners.

You need to be sure that you are creating engaging content that your followers will see of value. While you can post your sales and promotions, also post tweets with links to relevant blogs, articles, pictures and other information that can position you as a thought-leading expert who they need to continue to follow. Research your topic, provide valuable content. Be sure to use hashtags to find followers and partners. The hashtag (#) is used to mark specific words or topics within a Twitter post. Hashtags will increase your chance to have your message show up in a Twitter search, which helps reach potential customers who will find and follow your tweets.

It is important that you be consistent and post content on a regular basis. You will lose your followers if they are not seeing fresh content. But stay true to your strategy and post relevant posts that will keep your followers engaged and coming back to read your tweets. Use it to interact with your followers by sending direct private messages, thanking them when they write something positive. Share their messages in your tweets. Initiating two-way conversation will show that you are a real business and not a faceless company pushing product anywhere you can.

Because of the time that it does take to respond to feedback, you should prepare pre-developed responses for both positive and negative feedback. If someone makes a general statement such as they love your product, you can create a standard thank you response that anyone can post on the company's behalf. That will leave you time to respond to more specific questions and comments. It is important that you have pre-developed responses to negative feedback as well as the positive. An example would be if someone tweeted that it was the worst service they have ever had, a pre-developed response could be something like, "We apologize for the issue you have had. Can we follow up with you offline?" This shows that you are attempting to make sure that they know you are doing everything to correct the situation.

It is important, as with any medium you select to use for your business, that you track and measure traffic results. There are several tools you can use to do this – TweetReach and Google Analytics quantify how many sales are made from Twitter customers. If you set your website up correctly, you can use Google Analytics to measure who is coming to your site and what they are doing once there. Once you have this information, you can evaluate all your online tactics and measure what was the most effective form of communication and the best way of reaching people and when.

No matter which you chose to use – Twitter, LinkedIn or Facebook – you can, if you have budget, extend your reach and gain more followers by buying ad space. With Twitter, ads will allow you to promote your brand in search results and within the Twitter recommendation engine, and to be placed higher in the search results. LinkedIn offers self-service ads called LinkedIn Ads and customized ads calls LinkedIn Marketing Solutions. There are a number of places you can put ads in LinkedIn – InMails which appear in members' inboxes, polls, social ads in groups and timelines, and content ads. Facebook is beginning to offer options to promote your brand through content ads.

An element beginning to become more important to have in your brand toolkit is the use of video. Start with creating a video resume which should be a short video about you, your expertise and why you would be the best solution to their problem. Video marketing has proven itself as one of the most effective ways to market products online as it brings both a visual and an interactive element into marketing campaigns that can get lost with a static website. Plus, if done in a personal way where viewers see value, they are more likely to forward to others, so that your message and your brand grows virally.

You should consider several options, the most popular being YouTube, the largest video sharing site. This tool can really help grow your brand by getting your message out to a wide audience quickly. Create great headlines to get the viewers' attention to want to watch the full video, and want to share with others. Make sure the content is dynamic and interesting. The preview shot of a YouTube video is tied to the headline to increase your chance of getting a visitor to click on the play button and watch the rest of the video.

Be sure that you don't just post your videos on YouTube, but also host somewhere on your website. Content on your website is very important, and as video acts as content, it can be a valuable tool to boost conversions on your site. When creating your videos, make sure they provide real value, something of use to your customers and prospects.

As with other mediums discussed, monitor the activity on your video. Be sure to respond to any feedback posted in the comments section, especially when they are first posted. Measure and track results of visits to your videos using tools like Tube Mogul. Evaluate what you are posting and be sure, if you are going to use YouTube as one of your marketing tactics, that you post new videos on an ongoing basis to keep fresh and to increase your visibility.

As part of your video toolkit, you should considering the use of Podcasts. Podcasts have gained significant traction in recent years and are just video or audio recordings, distributed using RSS feeds where they can be downloaded by listeners to MP3 players, iPods, IPhones and computers. Like other mediums, this should fit into your overall strategy, with a specific goal for what you want to accomplish using Podcasts so that you know how they are performing, how they are helping you to grow your brand and your business. Goals can be that you want to use them to establish you as a thought-leading expert, to provide a service to customers and prospects, to promote a product, to attract new customers by giving them something of value without a sales pitch. Examples would be mini-seminars on subjects that show-case your expertise, provide interviews and industry news, tax tips, fitness tips, and provide features and benefits of a new product or service, and motivational messages.

Once you have decided that you want to use Podcasts, you need to think through format and length. Podcasts can go anywhere from one minute product overviews to fifteen minute tutorials and thirty minute interviews, either with a single person or multiple people. Consider your goal, what are you trying to achieve using Podcasts. Do you want to use them to demonstrate your product, how to use it, educate on a subject, provide tips and tricks? Once you have decided what you want them to do for you, determine the length and the frequency of your Podcasts. There are things to keep in mind when you are evaluating this as a tool in your kit. Video Podcasts take longer and require more equipment to prepare and edit than audio only.

If you want to do an interview, decide if it will be a stand-alone interview or will you do a series of interviews. Decide who you will interview and how are they viewed by your audience. Scheduling and interaction with your guests needs to be taken into consideration. First, you need to determine if you do it like a live radio show or pre-recorded only. A live recording takes more planning and requires a different platform to broadcast. They require background research. You need to prepare interview questions to guide the conversation. Decide what you will do when people reach out to be interviewed. Interviews can be very time consuming so carefully consider how this fits into your overall plan, and how much time you want to dedicate to it.

Determine the frequency for creating new Podcasts. While daily two-minute tips sound easy, it takes a great deal of time, discipline and content to make 365 recordings a year. It can take you up to thirty minutes or more to write and edit a tip concise enough to present in two minutes. Also, be sure to take into account the time to edit and prepare the Podcast to air.

Finally, and probably most important, is to plan your marketing. Just because you put together one of the best Podcasts, as with anything you put on the web, you have to promote it so that people know it's there and will download it, or you won't get many listeners and little to no value to all the effort you put into your Podcast. You need to be consistent, especially as you are trying to build your audience to listen on a regular basis. Put together a regular schedule of Podcasts and stick to it. You can create a number of them at one time and stage out the rollout of them so that you can quickly build a library. In order to build a regular audience, you need to commit to a schedule and stick to delivering it. Remember that your audience can listen to them wherever and whenever, but if you are not providing new content, they will unsubscribe you. While variety is good, know your audience, what they want to hear, and when they can download your Podcast.

With your limited time and resources, consider what you are trying to accomplish. For most people, reading is faster than listening to or watching video. It is believed that 10% to 15% of your targeted audience is actually going to listen to or watch Podcasts. You could have more people reading your newsletters and blogs than listening to your Podcasts. However, Podcasts are more engaging than reading because they can concentrate on your message, and they will take it with them in the car, on planes, trains, while working out, while waiting in line. Think of how many people you see with ear buds when they are out who you can reach with your Podcast but not necessarily with your printed materials. Video can become very viral and spread quickly if the message is relevant, and when appropriate, entertaining.

If, after you have evaluated this tool, you decide that you don't want to dedicate the time and energy to this medium, volunteer to be a guest on someone else's Podcast. That gives you the benefit of Podcasting without all the work, and gives you usable content that you can post on your website and link to in your postings.

There are many options and tools you can put into your toolkit to build your brand. Carefully consider your goals and what you are trying to accomplish. Build a roadmap of where you are starting and where you want to go. What are the stops along the way as you roll out new products and services that you want to build into your product offering. Once you have that, determine which of the tools are going to best help you achieve those goals and do them really well. Don't try to take on everything. Prioritize which elements are most important to you and build them. Once you feel like they are solid, you can add more elements.

Now, it's time to showcase to the world what you have built, and launch the brand called You.

Launching the Brand Called You

By giving people the power to share, we're mak-
ing the world more transparent.
Mark Zuckerberg, Facebook CEO

So, you now have your brand toolkit ready, and you are ready to go public with your brand. When you begin promoting your brand, it all matters. Everything you do communicates the character and the value of your brand. Everything from the way you interact with your customers and prospects, phone conversations, emails, to how you conduct yourself in meetings are all key elements of launching and establishing your brand. Every time someone forwards or shares one of your posts, your brand is being promoted.

Marketing should be viewed as a process, with steps, when followed, will enable you to execute a successful campaign. Key is to remember that the basic foundation of marketing and lead generation is message repetition. The more your target audiences hears and sees your message, the more they will remember your brand and will be confident that your brand is credible.

Building the right communication and launch plan is the first step to your success. Evaluate what elements you developed for your brand toolkit. Build a promotional plan to use all these elements, and at what point will you begin to bring others in and how you will incorporate them into your overall marketing strategy. A promotional plan involves key decisions about who the customer is, how to contact them, and what the message should be. Marketing communications include what you use to get your message out there and can be broken into several types.

Advertising is a mass media approach to communicating your message. This can include traditional elements like business directories, magazines and newspapers, TV and radio. You may use some of these elements at a local level in things like local magazines. However, these can be costly and out of reach for an early stage of your business.

Sales promotion is the use of coupons and discounts. Like the mass media approach, you can use local coupon books to give offers and discounts for customers and prospects to use or try your product or service. You can reward your frequent purchasers with additional discounts for repeat visits; offer higher incentives for first time buyers. You can anticipate about a 20% redemption rate. Most people will clip the coupon and forget to use it, or they will use it as a means of learning about what businesses have the services they are looking for. The challenge with coupons is that you either need to make them very attractive to get someone to contact you, or you advertised at the right time when they were looking for what you are offering.

One element most people don't use enough is the use of public relations as a means to promote and sell your brand. This includes press releases and events. Identify the local papers in your area that run local interest stories. Most have a business section. Many communities have local magazines or publications that will run feature articles. As you launch your business or introduce new product, write an article and send to these local papers and publications to gain exposure in your community to help spread your brand. Reach out to your local press and radio stations and invite them to your facility to make them your consumers and advocates. There is a lot of power in having them mention you, and you can get them to do it for free. Some stations and celebrities will even let you barter for free ad space in exchange for your product or service.

While it is important that you post these on your website, you need to make sure that you keep your press release section current and updated so that when people visit your site, they can see your progress and growth. While you can keep all your releases posted on your website, you don't want the most recent release to have been from two years ago.

Participate in community events as another means of using public relations to promote your brand. While you don't have to be a major sponsor, find ways that your brand can be featured at an event. Since you probably have limited resources and money, you want to be very strategic in what events you choose to participate in and at what level. Carefully consider the benefits to you and your brand in partnering with that event. While getting your name in the community is a good thing, at the end of the day, it is still about promoting your brand and growing your business. Determine which events you are passionate about that you want to do on a personal level and which make the most sense for your business. Marry the two where you can, but there may be times when you need to do events because they are near and dear to your heart and those that can help your business.

The next marketing communication element to consider is personal selling and can include trade shows, exhibitions, sales reps and showroom activities if you have a physical location. Not everyone has the desire or passion to sell. There are sales reps who will work for commissions only; and if there are other businesses in your market that may be offering complimentary services, you may consider sharing a sales resource. Agree what percent you are willing to pay this person for what they are able to sell for you, and give them the tools and the materials to sell your product. This frees you up to focus on the delivery and execution of your services.

Direct marketing, taking the message directly to the customer, is where your efforts in identifying your target market start to come into play. Direct marketing includes activities like direct mail, email, point of sale displays, packaging design, mail order catalogs and personalized letters. These typically have a cost with them that will need to be factored into your marketing budget. You can typically expect an average response rate of 3.4% for direct mail, though I have seen as high as 20% but that is the exception rather than the norm. According to Email Stats, as of 4Q2012, the average open rate for email is 27.4%, with an average click-through rate of 4.5% (**http://emailstatcenter. com/ResponseMetrics.html**). What that means is that if you send out 100 pieces of direct mail, you can expect to receive 4 calls, sending 100 emails means that 27 people will open your email, and two people will click to your ad or landing page. Other than advertising, this is the highest cost element that you can use, so it is important to make sure you have a very solid list of your target market audience that you are using for this element.

The final element is the use of digital marketing. This includes elements like your website, your social media strategy (Facebook, Twitter, and LinkedIn), blogging, YouTube, and ecommerce. You can accomplish a lot of brand building on social media with time, creativity and a little money. Over a billion people are using social media, presenting you with a lot of people to like your brand, and share it with their friends if they like you too. By using your time and creativity, you can market to people outside your direct connections and reinforce your brand in different contexts. We have already talked in several chapters about preparing for and using these channels, and these will most likely be the ones you predominately use to promote your brand and your products and services.

When thinking about how you will use the online channel to help promote you and your brand, some good options to consider are writing and posting free articles, video and podcast uploads, blogs, and promotional offers. Just posting messages to your Facebook, Twitter or LinkedIn will not build your brand unless what you post is focused on influencing the way your brand is perceived. You should focus not on being informative or valuable, but focus on changing perceptions and attitudes. That will help you build a stronger brand that people want to share with others. When your brand is working well on social media, it can seem like they see you in a lot of different places.

While Facebook is a very addictive medium, engagement is slowing down and showing signs of passive interaction. Users tend to log in, click apps, scroll through their wall, like pictures, sayings, videos, but then they close and move on. While there are still options like creating sponsored posts and posting viral thought provoking articles, your message can get lost in the mix, unless you pay to promote. Facebook should continue to be a part of your online media plan, but should no longer serve as your primary social platform to build your brand or your business.

One of social media's competitive advantages is the ability to be instant and very relevant. Part of your strategy should be prepared in advance so that you ensure a steady presence at a designated time, you need to be ready to be spontaneous and be prepared to react to your audience's attention in real time. Be aware of the "hot topics" including what they are watching on television, and to what they are listening. Brands that are able to be clever and most relevant will be recognized and rewarded. It is key that you know your brand inside and out so you can respond instantly, while staying true to your brand.

Gaining traction fast are Instagrams. While in its early stages, they are huge opportunities in this medium. Similar to Facebook, Instagrams are addictive in nature because of its exploring capabilities. Your customers start in one place, and next thing they know, they are clicking on artwork, which then leads to a purchase. Instagrams allow you to share your product or service, your company, and a link to your website.

There are quite a few online options, and more being added on a regular basis. What you decide to use will depend on the nature of your brand and your ability to execute, maintain and update. Don't try to take on every one of them at one time. Start with one of these and apply it in a meaningful way that will help you grow your brand and ultimately your business.

When you are starting a business and you don't have much to put against marketing your product or service, be sure that you are in strong position for Search Engine Optimization (SEO). With SEO, you are able to affect how visible your website is in search engines like Google and Bing. The higher placement you have on the page (or higher ranked on the search engines page), and the more frequently it appears in the search results list, the more visitors you will receive to your site. It is important when considering what content you want to put on your webpages, you need to keep your target audience in mind and have a good understanding of how they would search for you; what key words they would use. In order to optimize your website, you may need to revise your web content to increase relevance and to remove barriers of the indexing activities by the search engines.

One other thing I will mention is loyalty programs. You can use this to reward them for buying more of your product, frequently buying it or for generating referrals. While a strong loyalty program will enable you to market for less because you already have an existing relationship with that customer and you can get them to buy more from you, they can be time consuming to manage and administer. I would recommend that you really think through how you would handle fulfillment, and the life of the program. It can be hard to pull back on a loyalty program, and you do risk losing customers if you don't continue it or if you don't fulfill. It is much easier in a physical facility as you can give them a card that needs to be stamped, or some other means that makes the customer responsible for getting their reward. If you are a web-based business, it might be a little more difficult to manage, track and administer.

Deciding which medium, also known as media channels, to use is going to depend on your budget and what materials you have in your toolkit. All traditional media channels are now saturated, and competition for the consumer is very intense. Technology enables consumers to skip ads, and free information is now much more readily available. You will need to be very innovative in your approach to building your media plan. This is where your target marketing analysis comes into play when deciding what mediums to use to get the best bang for your buck, and stretch your dollars for maximum impact. Highly targeted efforts lead to better results. Personal letters perform better than general mailings. When deciding which media you want to use, consider what will have the greatest impact, what you can handle when responses come in, and how you will handle fulfillment.

Important to note is that once you have made your target market aware of your brand, you still need to guide them through the purchasing process. Identify the key steps the customer will have to take to get your products or services, and make sure communication is personalized and relevant during each step they go through.

Part of developing the promotional plan is answering key questions around who you are targeting and how you communicate with and talk to them. When they think about your brand, how do you want them to perceive it? You should understand what their media consumption habits are, where they go for information, what are their buying habits, expectations, habits, priorities. Knowing what kind of disposable income they have will help to know what they are willing to pay for your product or service. This information can be obtained by looking at their social media interactions and website statistics. If you have any type of "opted in" email distribution list, you can send out surveys through free tools like Survey Monkey and Zoomerang. An opted in email address means that the recipient has agreed to receive emails from you.

Once you have a good picture of your potential customer, it's time to work on getting their attention. You need to determine what your objective is. Are you trying to generate awareness for your new brand, attract new business or grow your prospect list? Your message points should address your target group, talk the way they talk, focus on their pain points and how what you are offering will help them. Make it about them, not about you and your brand. How can you help them solve their problem? How do you make life easier for them? Regardless of whether you are promoting your brand, a new product or raising awareness, it is important that the message you use works across all medium, and that they work together towards a common goal by using similar messaging and "look and feel". Using an integrated approach can dramatically increase the effectiveness of any marketing campaign and will help create your brand image.

To get the best response rates, you need to ensure that your message is relevant and clear. Once you have managed to get the attention of your target audience, you need to make sure that you have a clear, concise message that they understand and react to what you are saying. Your call to action should be easy to find and should include what you want them to do once they read and are interested in your offer. Do you want them to visit your website, and once there, is it clear what they need to do to get the offer. If you give them a number to call, consider staffing hours and include that in your message. You may want to think about how you handle calls immediately following your message being served.

When developing your message, it should fall into three main categories: to inform about your brand and products, and should be used to help you develop a competitive advantage. To persuade them to respond instantly to your message and/or your offer, and should be used to drive sales. To remind your target audience about your brand and products so that you stay top of mind when they are in the market for your products or services.

A good exercise to start with when developing your message is to develop a creative brief. A creative brief will help you define the purpose, what you want to communicate, what each element will do and how you plan to incorporate them together. A creative brief is an outline of what you want delivered and includes a description of the task, background on the company or product, target audience, main message you want communicated and timeline. Typically an ad agency uses these to kick off a project as it concisely provides the direction needed to create the work, and ensures everyone is on the same page before resources are assigned. Even if you are not using an agency, it is still a good exercise to start any creative process with this document to make sure that you think through what you want to say, how you want to say it and to whom. When you don't have a complete grasp of what you are trying to communicate, it's hard for your creative team to create and effectively tell your story.

A creative brief is not a lengthy report, but more like a spec sheet for the job. There are nine sections to a creative brief. It is typically a one to two page document.

First, you need to define the project deliverables – what you want created. This is good to do when you are working with a designer to create your website, when you create videos, an email campaign, and a newsletter.

Second is to identify the expectations for this project. This includes considerations like increasing followers, website visits, click to subscribe to a newsletter or to even buy your product or service. It is what action you want people to take when they see your marketing efforts.

The third piece is to provide a clear description of your target market. This should include demographics, psychographics, as well as how you think the audience currently knows and feels about what you are offering, and what they know about your brand.

Once you have identified these key elements, you need to help your creative team, or for yourself, what message you want to send to your targeted audience. This should be based on how you have defined your brand, what you want your brand to say about you, how you want to be represented, and your particular products and services being offered. When they see your message, what do you want them to think or feel about you and your products? This is often defined as the essence of the brand identity and should describe the emotion you want the audience to feel when they see your ads and messages.

One important element you need to provide is the justification or the support for the statements you are making. Your audience needs to know why they should believe what you are claiming. This is your opportunity to detail the benefits of your product or service, why you are the better choice over other options available to them. Be sure to define your brand promise and make sure that everything you say represents that promise. Never lose sight of what you want to be to your customers. Every piece of communication should tie back to your brand identity.

You do need to define considerations and restrictions. These are things like length preference of a video, the number of videos you want created, the words and phrases that must be said or things that cannot be said. Include whether there are any cost restrictions or pre-requisites before they can buy one service.

Once you have completed this document, you are ready to start developing your creative. As you complete each element, compare it to your creative brief to make sure that you are consistent in what you are saying across all elements. Make sure to use the same font, colors and logo usage in each of your elements.

Branding is a powerful tool for positioning your product. It is very important that you include your branding on all elements used, and should be consistent – the same logo, colors, font, message. You want your target audience to see you in different forms, but you want them to say the same things about you when they see you in different places. Besides, it is difficult unless you hire someone to handle for you, to manage different messages in different places. That being said, you do need to tailor for your medium being used so some tweaking may be required, but your overall message, look and feel should be the same everywhere.

In order to gain awareness of your brand, to sell your product and to grow your business, you will need to advertise at some point. Whatever you are planning to use to accomplish this, you need to go through the same process every time. Be sure that you know your audience, target them efficiently and effectively, and position your brand in a manner that you stand out in the crowd.

When evaluating what channels you want to use, keep in mind that there are many free avenues to get your message out there, engage consumers and give you a higher return on your investment for your paid efforts. Probably the two best ones to use are public relations and online.

Measuring for Success

"If you can't measure it, you can't manage it."
Peter Drucker, Consultant, Education and Author

Your goal in marketing your brand, products and service is to sell more of what you are offering, to remain relevant and recognizable. You can create what you think is a solid marketing communications plan, but if you don't measure the effectiveness of each of the elements, you won't be able to determine what worked, what you should do more or less of. Traditional marketing elements– TV, radio, newspaper – are difficult to measure without some type of research on how the message was perceived and understood, did it resonate, what caused them to respond. Research can be costly and still won't help you know what your true response rate was to each of those elements.

Measuring brand impact is not an easy task. While you can measure clicks, calls, and sales, it is difficult to tell which medium, or combination of, is changing your follower's attitudes about your brand, or if they remember your business name when they are looking for a solution to their problem or for what service you offer. You can't assume that every sale is a result of your last marketing campaign. It is the combination of all your efforts; every time you reach someone, you further build brand recall. If you credit any one tactic as the reason why people responded or bought your product or service, you may be missing out on how they all work together, and how you need to use multiple ways to reach your target audience.

Digital marketing is very different than traditional media and is very measurable. There are two ways to measure your brand impact through digital marketing. Think of this as being the amount of advertising space your brand occupies compared to the amount of advertising space your target audience may be exposed to. These include your ad impressions, the total number of times your ads are displayed to everyone who visits the website your ad is featured on, and ad frequency, the number of times your ads are displayed during a given time period. The more people see your ads, the more likely they will remember your brand.

As you build your website, you need to set up web analytics to figure out what people are doing when they come to your website. Web analytics should provide you with feedback on what you need to change or do to enhance what people are seeing when they come to your website. Things to look at include how long are they spending on your site, what pages do they click to, how long do they stay on those pages, how many pages do they look at before they take action. Remember, your website should be treated as a living, breathing tool that you should be working to update to improve the customer experience. Google Analytics provides free tools for you to do this.

You can measure how your brand is growing by seeing an increase in the number of people searching for your company, the increase in traffic to your website and leads. One way to gather leads is to create a form page on either your website or your landing page. When you see an increase in form conversions on either of these, you can measure your brand lift.

Action metrics track how your target audience reacts when they see your ad and is measured through three measurements. The number of clicks your ad receives is the click-through rate. The number of people who take immediate action after seeing your ad is your post-click conversion. While not everyone takes immediate action when seeing your ad, many do come back at a later time and download your white paper, sign up for a free trial or buy from you; this is a post-impression conversion. While many think that measuring the value of your campaign by tracking the clicks on your ad, the leads generated and the amount spent on your ad, you will end up trying to optimize your ads to get the lowest cost per click and lowest cost per action. The more valuable approach to tracking clicks is to focus on those clicks that drive purchasing, not just clicks. Having someone download a white paper, fill out a form to capture their information and building your lead list is far more valuable than someone just clicking on your ad.

Mistakes are not mistakes if you learn from them. If you try something and it does not drive the results that you were hoping for, spend time analyzing the data afterwards to see what worked and what did not. You need to be willing to take risks and decide when something is good enough. Extra time you spend perfecting things could cost you money in the long run. A good example of this is Fab.com. Seventy percent of their revenue is generated by email. If they spent one extra day perfecting an email campaign rather than sending something good enough, the company could lose $700K in lost revenue. You need to learn when you can trust your instincts that it is right. Watch closely and be prepared to adjust, but give it time before pulling.

If you are a new business, you should be looking at customer insights and adjusting your approach as you learn more about what works and what doesn't. While still staying consistent with your brand look and feel, you can test different messages to see what gets the best response. This is easier to do in the digital space. With display advertising, even on a limited budget, you can test several versions since you can buy either on a cost-per-click (CPC) or a cost-per-impression (CPM) basis. With cost per click, you focus on maximizing the number of clicks. CPM allows you to focus your ad creative and your display campaign more on the brand impact than trying to drive a huge number of clicks that might not result in anything.

When I launch new products, I have several different banner ads created, each pulling out a different feature or benefit of the product to see which one people clicked on. By using targeted efforts, putting your ads where your prospects and customers go, you can see what is important to them, and what they are most likely to respond to. If you don't get the response you are looking for, try again with a different message, different placement. You can keep testing until you find the right formula for your business.

Branding is something that you have to focus on a continuous basis. You can't just put it out there and expect people to find you. You need to create ad content that matters to your audience and gets them to take the action you want them to take. While possible, you most likely will not get it right on the first try. You will need to try different things – different messages, ads, images – to see what is going to work for you. Testing is one way to see what is going to work for you, and is very simple to do.

In order to test your ad creative, the best way to do this is to create two or three different versions of the same ad creative. This can be done by varying offers to see what works best. You can try, for example, a 30-day trial, a 90-day trial or a customer testimonial about using your product. Run all ads at the same time, then compare which ad performs the best to see what offer and messaging works best with your target audience.

An example of this that I recently read about was how the travel site TripAdvisor.com tests new feature concepts by placing dummy banner ads on their site to test different features the company is thinking about offering. If a visitor clicks on the banner, they take them to a "404 Page Not Found" message. They use that as a gauge to determine whether enough visitors clicked on the banner. The company will then start to develop that product to take to market. This saves them considerable dollars over the traditional methods of conducting focus groups and doing research.

You can do the same thing on your website to see what type of interest people have in a particular service you are thinking of offering. A word of caution though, you don't want to overuse them or people will stop coming to your site as they will get frustrated that they get error messages whenever they visit. I would recommend that you only use it for major changes or additions to what you are currently offering.

Whatever type of analysis that you do or have provided to you, be sure that you take action. A 50-page report detailing campaign performance is only useful if you use it to determine what you will do differently next time you do the campaign. Don't get wrapped up in trying to interpret the data, reviewing campaigns for weeks without coming up with action steps on how you are going to improve and grow. Rather than reporting dozens of statistics, focus on a few that will tell you whether your campaign is working, and what you might need to change in the future to make it more successful. Don't be afraid to test and try new things, but be sure to measure and track them to see what is working

Your campaigns should only take days to roll out. During the initial roll out, you should carefully monitor how it is performing, what is working and what you need to change. If you are using multiple mediums, determine where traffic is coming from. Are you getting more clicks on your website, a banner ad you placed on Google, or more calls and foot traffic from the local coupon book? Small changes can lead to saved time and better performance in the long run, resulting in more sales.

It does take time to measure the true impact of what you are doing. While you want to monitor how your current campaign is performing, you don't want to look at one single effort. You want to make sure that you compare your results from each of your efforts. Measure how you are building your brand awareness. Do more people know about your brand and are they following you. Evaluate if you have changed the attitudes and preferences of your followers over longer periods of time.

There are a tools that you can use to monitor and measure how your brand and your messages are performing. You don't have to use all of these tools. You should use those that are related to the marketing element most important to your marketing strategy. To monitor your overall brand, you can use Social Mention, one of the most powerful brand monitoring tools available. Social Mention (found at socialmedia.com) is a social media platform that aggregates content you put together across multiple platforms – Twitter, Facebook, LinkedIn, YouTube among others – into a single stream of information. It allows you to directly link to any activity that mentions you and your brand, and if used properly, can help you present yourself as natural, responsive and personable.

Through Google Alerts, you can monitor your news and blogs. While these will be picked up with Social Mention, Google Alerts is tailored for blogs and news outlets. Simply plug in whatever topic you want to track, and Google Alerts will email you updates, automatically keeping you up to date on anything related to your brand.

Another aggregation service is FriendFeed, which is most useful as a networking tool and as a way to track your competition. It builds a social network around the content it aggregates. FriendFeed allows you to put all your and your friends' feeds in one place, comment on other people's feeds and be part of the conversation and helps you to consolidate and reinforce your social network.

A tool called BrandYourself is an easy way to control how you show up in search engines. It will help you optimize your website and social network for maximum search rankings. They do offer a basic service package for free that will allow you to improve your Google results. It is simple to use. You just need to tell them what links you want to rank and the tool will tell you how to make it happen.

Keep your customers in the driver's seat

"In this ever-changing society, the most powerful and enduring brands are built from the heart. They are real and sustainable. Their foundations are stronger because they are built with the strength of the human spirit, not an ad campaign. The companies that are lasting are those that are authentic."
- Howard Schultz, CEO and Chairman, Starbucks

As you go through the process of defining and building your brand, always keep your customer at the forefront of everything you do. Without them, you don't have a business. With all of the new apps, websites, social networks, and trying to keep up with all the new places that you could get your message out, it is sometimes easy to forget that what motivates people remains the same. What they really want out of life, what they want from you doesn't change as technology does. Step back and make sure that you look at what your customers really want from you. Make sure you know what they really care about and what is motivating them to purchase from your company.

People like to connect with real people. Before you can position your brand across multiple channels, you need to be very clear as to why people should engage with you in the first place. Define your mission. Be very clear why they should choose you. Targeting your marketing becomes easier to do when you sharpen the purpose behind your approach. Stay true to your brand, what you stand for, and you will be more likely to see sales, new customers, new clients coming in, and increasing rates as you build out your brand.

Many tend to start a business without realizing how really difficult it is to actually create a successful business. Just because you tell your friends and family that you have started a business will you be ensured success. In fact, it will only take you so far. Take time to learn about marketing, create a plan you can implement and be willing to either hire or find someone who can do the things that you can't or are unwilling to do.

Be sure to use an integrated approach for the best results. Using just one technique is helpful, but you won't see the results that you really want when you depend on just one way to drive your traffic. Don't be afraid to test multiple tactics with different messages to see what performs the best. People respond to different messages placed in multiple locations. It is no longer about chasing after prospects but developing relationships and attracting customers to you, by providing useful resources and positive experiences for your target audience.

Your growth is about people. Think ahead and prepare for scalability. Always be thinking about what happens when your business grows to the plus-one more than you can currently handle. Have a plan for growth.

You may be spending a lot of time generating leads, but do you have time to work those leads? Don't let them grow cold because you can't get to them fast enough, or you don't have a plan to turn them into sales for your company. Prepare the steps in between for how you are going to deal with each lead as it comes in. Have a back-up plan if you have the good fortune of attracting more leads than you planned, and conversely, one if you don't get as many as you planned to get. As you go through the process of developing and executing your marketing plan, be sure to know how you are going to handle the sales side of it. Both sales and marketing need to be ongoing processes, each requiring dedicated time and attention.

The web provides an invaluable, unique marketing tool to promote your business. Use it to your full advantage by efficiently setting up automatic email responders, prescheduling your Tweets to Twitter, and posts to blogs, Facebook and LinkedIn. Frequent social media updates have the added benefit of driving more traffic and attention from visitors and search engines. Use your website to prescreen customers, answer frequently asked questions, and to provide downloadable materials including sales kits, marketing brochures and press materials.

Consumers are searching with more specificity than ever before. To be found online, you need to include specific content on your website. Be sure to have the details of what you want people to buy from you on your site. If your products or services do not show up in search results when consumers are looking for them, you risk losing them to your competition that does have the information on what they for and shows up in the search. Remember, when it comes to social media, content is king. Without interesting content, your brand is not noticed. Content is no longer about text on the page, but comes from a combination of videos, short stories, testimonials, facts and strong visuals.

No longer are your claims or guarantees enough to promote conversion from leads to sales. Today's consumer is resourceful, Internet-savvy, and more dependent than ever before on customer reviews, page rankings, and other distributed opinions. You need to be able to prove your value over and over to keep your customers returning, and to help you grow new ones. Be authentic and credible. Provide real-life stories. Get your customers to give you testimonials about their experience with you.

You don't need to spend a lot on advertising. Relying on tools like Google and Facebook where you can specifically target your audience and see if your ads are working within a few days, costs less than $100.

There is a lot to think about and consider in defining, building and launching a brand. Be sure to take it one step at a time. Take the time upfront to really define who and what you want your brand to be. What you want people to say, think and do when you come their mind. Once you can clearly articulate you, the who and what, determine what you want that to look like, your brand personality. The more time you spend to create a clear vision and definition for yourself, the easier it will be to communicate that and get your potential customers aware of who you are and why they should buy from you.

There are so many options available today to promote you and your brand. Choose wisely which ones you know that you can sustain on an ongoing basis. Putting up a Facebook page that you never touch does not build credibility or reliability in the eyes of your followers, so they will question whether you will fulfill what you promise. Your customers should always be the drivers for how you build and evolve your business.

Building your brand is not a one-time exercise, but one that needs to continually be nurtured, massaged, and evolve as you and your business grows, as your roles change. The more in tune you are with your customers, how they are reacting to you, how they communicate with you, what they think of you, the easier that evolution becomes. You are your own brand. You are a one of a kind brand. No one is like you. Define it, own it, be it. You are the brand called You.

Resources

The following resources were used in the development of this book.

Emerging Technologies Demand New Marketing Fundamentals: Marketers Who Try to Respond with Today's Practices and Skills Will Fail

By: Anthony Mullen

Published: March 04, 2013

Four Ways to Market Like a Startup

by Brian Gregg and Vivian Weng | 9:00 AM March 22, 2013

http://blogs.hbr.org/cs/2013/03/four_ways_to_market_like_a_sta. html?goback=%2Egde_51822_member_225547698

Build A Personal Brand, Not Just A Career

http://www.forbes.com/sites/lisaquast/2012/11/19/ build-a-personal-brand-not-just-a-career/

Personal Branding 101: How to Discover and Create Your Brand

http://mashable.com/2009/02/05/personal-branding-101/

3 Steps To Build Your Personal Brand For Tomorrow's Business (Tips From The CIO)

http://www.forbes.com/sites/netapp/2013/02/06/
cio-personal-branding/

How to Build Your Personal Brand

http://www.wikihow.com/Build-Your-Personal-Brand

8 Tips for Building Your Brand on the Cheap

http://mashable.com/2012/09/10/cheap-branding/

Lauren Drell Sep 10, 2012

How to Build a Strong Brand

http://www.marketing-made-simple.com/articles/brand-building.htm

Freelancer's Guide to Building a Brand Identity from Scratch

http://freelanceswitch.com/start/brand-identity-from-scratch/

The Brand Called You

By Tom Peters

http://www.fastcompany.com/28905/brand-called-you

About Debbie Cummings

I have spent more than 25 years as a marketing professional, developing marketing and branding strategies, planning and executing new product launches and initiating targeted marketing initiatives. I have worked on products and brands for companies like Procter & Gamble, Cellular One, Cincinnati Bell, ZoomTown, TKR Cable, InterMedia Cable, Bright House Networks, Hermann Engelmann Greenhouses Exotic Angels, and even a short stint in the Cayman Islands for the cable operator there. Though some you may never have heard of, they are big companies, brands with big budgets, launching a lot of different products all the time.

My initial brand training began at Procter & Gamble, a company known for its strong brands, initially in the patent office, working on products from the initial concept phase and then moving into product research running diaper studies. I learned so much about market research and branding. While a great company and an industry leader in branding, recruiting babies was not exactly what I wanted to spend my career doing, so I left the consumer packaged goods world to move into the more entrepreneurial world of telecommunications.

My first job in telecommunications was working for Cellular One in 1987. It was very early days in the wireless industry. Back then, it was about selling airtime minutes. Phones started at $999 and went to as high as almost $4,000. I started as marketing coordinator, and while I had so much fun going to events and introducing cellular phones, it was challenging to create marketing campaigns for something people had no clue about. It was not just about building a brand, but convincing people why they needed a phone at that price and that they had to pay per minute. I honed my retail skills when I moved into a Retail/Dealer Manager position, launching the first cellular retail program in the Dayton area.

As a side note, I was one of the first of my family and friends to have a cell phone. It was one of the brick phones and it was very heavy, but I was so cool going around talking on my cell phone. I did get funny looks though when they installed the first hands-free system into my car and I drove around in my car just talking away.

Then I caught the cable television bug. Renegade days of early cable when people would chase the trucks to get service installed. Early days when you are the only game in town was a marketer's dream. I launched new channels, new equipment, new packages and offers. I built a brand at a time when no one really knew why they should have to pay for programming, coming from a world of 3 channels, 4 in some markets. I advanced through a series of promotions that led to roles like Regional Marketing Director for the Western Kentucky region for InterMedia Communications, Managing Director at Cincinnati Bell, Corporate Business Marketing Director at Bright House Networks, and finally Senior Marketing Executive at WestStar in the Cayman Islands.

As strategic marketing professional, I have proven my ability to build and develop brands, identify unique opportunities and increase revenues. I have a demonstrated track record of driving strong marketing campaign response rates and execution of successful product launches. I have developed and launched integrated print, web and direct marketing campaigns, increased brand awareness, developed collateral and training brochures, and countless product launches. I have been acknowledged as the recipient of several Awards of Excellence and winning Marketer of the Year for outstanding marketing initiatives and growth.

I earned my MBA, specializing in e-Business, from the University of Phoenix, as an early adopter of using technology as a learning tool, and have a Bachelor of Arts in Public Relations from Eastern Kentucky University. I am an AFAA certified Personal Trainer and a JNL Master Certified Trainer.

I have two amazing sons, Stephen and Sean, and two wonderful rescue dogs, Juno and Janey.